I GIVE YOU MY WORD

I GIVE YOU
MY WORD

by

IVOR BROWN

JONATHAN CAPE
THIRTY BEDFORD SQUARE
LONDON

FIRST PUBLISHED NOVEMBER 1945
SECOND IMPRESSION SEPTEMBER 1946

PRINTED IN GREAT BRITAIN IN THE CITY OF OXFORD
AT THE ALDEN PRESS
BOUND BY A. W. BAIN & CO. LTD., LONDON

INTRODUCTION

THE appearance of a third book in what is becoming, rather formidably, a succession of verbal anthologies, is due to two facts. First, people, in numbers agreeably surprising to me, appear to like this kind of thing: second, they confirm and express that liking by sending in copious comments and suggestions for future volumes. In my second book *Just Another Word* and in the double volume which included that and its predecessor, *A Word in Your Ear*, I included lists of my correspondents together with my thanks for this help and encouragement. I naturally and cordially continue to state my gratitude in general, but this time I must apologize for not printing new lists of names. Not only have they become multitudinous: but also, any register of mine would now be incomplete owing to the difficulty I have had in keeping my correspondence and notes together and in order. Anyone who shared the experience of endeavouring to write and work systematically in London and south-east England during the year, especially the late summer, of 1944 will understand what I mean.

So I must simply apologize to my benefactors and leave the list out, since it would be grossly discourteous to mention some names and omit others, whose owners may have given me equal or even greater assistance. Many have sent me 'family words', amusing and vivid, or dialect words of an extremely localized type. Plainly a collection of these would soon outrun all limits. I am glad to hear about them and I have mentioned a few such, because I refuse to be bullied by my own rules. But one must be sparing with these gifts lest the main purpose be interrupted. That purpose has been to show the richness of the English which has, or has had, what may be called Dictionary Status. To admit all private coinage and all dialect creations would open the gates too widely and the result would be an enormous collection of picturesque oddities rather than the balanced anthology of likeable and useable terms, with quotations to match, which it was my original ambition to create. I wanted the collection to be fun: I also wanted it to be, in some sort, fruitful.

My previous prefaces included some disquisition on the abuses and absurdities of contemporary English writing, especially in official documents. I do not propose this time to write a further treatise on the wounds and tumours which afflict our language with scarcely any diminution, perhaps even increasingly. What is horrifying is that writers of repute allow this officialese to seep in and clog their own vocabulary. The silly habit, for example, of refusing to call the poor the poor is practised more and more. That the poor we have always with us is translated (even in literary journals) into some ponderosity about the permanence in the social structure of the under-privileged and lower income groups. The sick are no longer cured and sent home. They are now dehospitalized with a view to psycho-physical rehabilitation in domestic surroundings. My correspondents supply me with plentiful horrors of this kind, and I can find abundance of odious verbal pomposity for myself. One great motor-bus company in the North of England, as I have myself noticed when travelling, was eager to give some sensible advice to travellers and insisted on calling this counsel 'Busology'. I suppose the name was devised by one of those people who nowadays never talk about a man's opinions or beliefs, but always about his reactions and his ideology. The odious and absurd habit of making new verbs out of nouns derived from verbs (e.g. to signature) gets steadily worse. 'To reference' is the latest silliness of this kind to which I have been introduced. 'This was referenced to a speech earlier in the debate.'

This kind of word-play undoubtedly pleases some of those who use it (many do so out of sheer laziness and habit) and it will not soon or easily be stopped. Indeed, extending popular education will probably aggravate matters, at least for the time being, by turning out myriads with just enough book-learning to judge words by their number of syllables as others judge cars by their number of cylinders. This kind of verbal sciolism is a natural

6

foppery of the young idea: I would like to think that the older we grow, the simpler our words. But that does not markedly happen. I scarcely expect to see verbosity dwindle. What we can hope to do is to keep alive, as far as may be, old, vigorous English (and Scottish), rescuing the brief and burly, the rare and exquisite words, along with muscular and pointed phrases, whether they be an antique heritage or of recent minting.

Mention of Scotland reminds me that I have been criticized by some of my correspondents for bringing in Scottish words too frequently. That I may have used Scottish terms less in this volume is accidental (I have been reading fewer Scottish books). As the dedication of this volume suggests, I remain impenitent about their rightful place in such an anthology. Scotland still has three languages, Gaelic, surviving sparsely in the Highlands and more thickly in the islands, the official and normal English imposed by the conquerors and properly accepted and used for utility reasons by most educated Scots, and the 'Lallans', as it is now fashionable to call the popular speech of the Lowlands and the eastern counties. Of the Lallans many genteel Scots used to be ignorant and ashamed, except on Burns Night and on similar occasions of rather a self-conscious release for repressed nationalistic sentiment. But there is now a realization, especially among the younger Scottish writers, that this is a powerful and, in many ways, beautiful language deserving a fate far kinder than preservation in a literary museum. A gifted and many-tongued Scot like Douglas Young writes poetry in Lallans just as much, and just as well, as he does in Gaelic, English, Latin, Greek, French, and German. Such men regard Lallans not merely as a speech once fruitfully used by Ramsay and Burns, but as a surviving and valuable member of a comity of tongues. I agree with them.

Furthermore the Lallans is not Scottish only. Its kinship with Northern English (and the many derivations of both from Scandinavian roots and terms) is plain. The curious slanting line which marks the Anglo-Scottish border is an accident of history, a history so largely composed of family feuds. The countryside on both sides of it is similar and so are the occupations and habits of the people.

7

In the hills they farm sheep: in the plains and dales they get coal and other minerals. The difference in economy and tradition between Scotland's Hawick and Yorkshire's Hawes is far less than the difference between Yorkshire's Hawes and Sussex Horsham. The tumble of fells running from the Peak to the Pentlands is a unity and the speech of its people has considerable unity too. I was lately reading a book of Cumbrian folk-songs and tales. Its lingo was as near to the Lallans as Carlisle to Ecclefechan. As I said before, I do not want these books of mine to become just repositories of obscure dialect forms. But Lallans, as a tongue, is neither dead nor diminutive: it is closely intermingled with Northern English: it is having its own great Dictionary slowly (all too slowly!) prepared: it has lived in a literature of its own and is increasingly renewing that life. So I shall take leave to neglect these English scoldings and quote Scottish vocabulary when I choose.

Many of my letters have come from schoolmasters. I am glad of this, for it shows their affection for the element in which they do much of their work. It is needless to remark upon the enormous responsibility for the safeguarding and strengthening of language which lies upon the shoulders, the already much-burdened shoulders, of teachers. They can do so much to quicken young intelligence and sensibility by their own choice of words and by their comment on the words of others. 'Eng. Lit.' may be the most dismal of drudgeries for all when there is a dull or bored teacher; but it is bliss for the gifted pupil, and should indeed be enjoyable by all the class, if the man or woman at the desk or dais feels the persuasion of good writing and can explain it, showing how the simplest words are raised to a higher power by selection, stress, and combination.

It is customary and proper in prefaces to books to acknowledge the helpfulness of other books. I would like to carry the obligation further back and (justly, I think) salute the people who first brought me to those books and made them seem friendly instead of formidable. To put young people on easy terms with the arts is the first business of a good teacher and those who do it deserve infinite gratitude. Our pastors and masters do not get much in the way of acclamation from those whom they herded along the educational highway or propelled up the academic ladder. So I would like to break the general rule of neglect by thanking three of them who brought me to the liking of language.

At Cheltenham College I had for Sixth Form master W. N. Weech, later Head Master of Sedbergh, and then a recent product of Winchester and New College, to the ripe culture of which foundations he added a personal relish for wit and a particular zest for a well-filed epigram. He liked the sardonic and to the rendering of Tacitus brought the finest taste in the diamond phrase that cut and sparkled. F. R. G. Duckworth, who became His Majesty's Senior Inspector of Schools, taught essay-writing with a lounging, easy-going manner in sharpest contrast to the speed and crispness of Weech. But his seeming fatigue was the cloak for an immense devotion to English and of an active zeal for the better use of it. He wrote finely himself and was a contributor on the ardours and endurances of pedagogy to the old *Morning Post*, then a-glitter with the work of such stylists as Belloc and Maurice Baring, in whose company he could take a natural place. He went on to Eton and later was so heavily engaged in the cares of educational administration and inspection that he wrote far too little. He introduced me to and made me at home with a grand variety of authors from Robert Browning to Robert Blatchford. His domestic Sunday evenings, with refreshment, the Muses, and a friendly wit, were charming hospitality and made a most welcome break in the too rigid routine of school-life as it then was. I hope that he will renew his old practice of writing in his new-gained leisure.

An earlier and even larger debt is to F. J. Cade, the remarkable Head for many years of Cheltenham's Junior School. I came into his Upper Fourth at the age of eleven and stayed there until I could go to the Senior, nearly three years later. Cade was a disciple of F. W. H. Myers, much concerned about Intimations of Immortality, and able to make the smallest boy aware that Wordsworth's Ode meant something real. He would quote Tennyson's 'In Memoriam' with haunting power, ruminating aloud on the use of finely sounding words and of alternate alliteration. I can hear him now proclaim,

> His heavy-shotted hammock-shroud
> Drops in a vast and wandering grave

and then comment on the emotional power of the lettering, especially of the 'a's in the second line. He was my first guide to Vergil and naturally his zest for brave, translunar (or at least *post mortem* things) made him choose the sixth book of the Aeneid. At the age of eleven or twelve one moves rather slowly on these heights (or more exactly in these Avernian depths). We prepared but twenty or thirty lines at a time, but he made the task, in the true sense, thrilling. He made one's senses quiver at the poetry. It is not easy, I fancy, to awaken really young minds in the poignance of *ripae ulterioris amore* or to make them responsive to the colour and throb of the great Vergilian hexameters as they surge to the subterranean sublimities of Aeneid VI. Cade, a man of small, dark, piercing eyes that seemed to look beyond this world of matter, an invalid and I think in some ways morbid of mind as of body, had the true genius of the teacher. When he opened a book, he opened one's eyes. He drove at sense and fancy. His lessons were a lesson.

I make these salutes to individual men. But I feel that most people who enjoy their reading to-day must owe something, perhaps far more than they realize, to a teacher who could light up a line of poetry or explain just why certain sayings, as well as certain doings, vibrate in the memory. So, by secondary purpose, my salute is public and general and goes to any dominie or directress of studies who has ever carried the young idea beyond the task-work to the treasuring of 'stuff in books'. I understand, I hope, the dangers of making schooling a sentimental journey. There has to be the task-work and I think we shall lose a great deal by flying in panic from the old, fair-and-square examination system because of the application and hard work which it involves. (The alternative is nomination, based on general impressions of a thing vaguely called 'character' which is bound to let in all kinds of snobbery and jobbery and make the world safe for bone-headed athletes, muscular Christians, prudent little prigs and other forms of head-masters' pets.) Of course, it is quite possible for the examination system to turn out the crammed, quickly-responding type who thinks only in terms of right answers and high marks and would make the poets and orators mere rungs in the ladder of his career. But the balance is in the old system's favour and there have been, are, and still surely will be plenty of teachers who can enable their pupils to get true pleasure from a poet as well as ninety marks out of a hundred. These are the men and women in whose hands our bounteous inheritance of words so largely lies. To them every writer should be grateful, since they determine the quality of his audience. And not writers only. The essence of living is the power of appreciation, the savouring of thoughts and things. He who does not enjoy does not live. If teachers are themselves good tasters and relishers of the feast and can transmit their zest to others, they are rarely gifted and great benefactors. Much do we owe them.

I am again much indebted to my friend and colleague, J. C. Trewin, for his vigilant scrutiny of my quotations, and to Miss Allen, Miss Catt, and Miss Attwood for secretarial help generously given at a time when they had plenty of toil and trouble on their hands.

To my fellow-Scot

JAMES BRIDIE

who writes our two languages with
equal fancy, vigour, and felicity

ABHOR

FOR writers of the sixteenth and seventeenth century abhor was a word of abundant fascination. Justly, for it expresses a shrinking aversion with such power. The Bible is full of this vivid loathing.

> 'If I wash myself with snow water', cried Job, 'and make my hands never so clean: yet shalt thou plunge me in the ditch and mine own clothes shall abhor me.'

Oddly, ditch and abhorrence are words again linked in Cleopatra's tremendous refusal of surrender.

> Shall they hoist me up,
> And show me to the shouting varletry
> Of censuring Rome? Rather a ditch in Egypt
> Be gentle grave unto me! rather on Nilus' mud
> Lay me stark-naked, and let the water-flies
> Blow me into abhorring! rather make
> My country's high pyramides my gibbet,
> And hang me up in chains.

The deep roll of its second syllable gives macabre power to the word abhorring. Students of alliteration can ponder on Shakespeare's majestic drum-beats of 'r' and 'm' both here (especially in the penultimate lines) and in the famous passage in *Romeo and Juliet*.

> Ah, dear Juliet,
> Why art thou yet so fair? shall I believe
> That unsubstantial Death is amorous,
> And that the lean abhorrèd monster keeps
> Thee here in dark to be his paramour?
> For fear of that, I still will stay with thee;
> And never from this palace of dim night
> Depart again: here, here will I remain
> With worms that are thy chamber-maids; O, here
> Will I set up my everlasting rest;

And shake the yoke of inauspicious stars
From this world-wearied flesh. — Eyes, look your last!
Arms, take your last embrace!

'R', always so cogent, is the dominant letter: the 'm's assist. The number of 'r's and 'm's in this passage is worth counting. Abhorred is the perfect adjective for monster and the paramour in the next line echoes the triple music of o, r, and m.

For that were Idolatry to be abhorred of all faithful Christians.

The word is so much stronger than hated. If the Rubric has not kept all Christians from idolatry, no phrase could more formidably have striven to do so.

But the fair guerdon when we hope to find,
And think to burst out into sudden blaze,
Comes the blind Fury with th' abhorrèd shears
And slits the thin-spun life.

Milton's lines have always haunted me: the abhorréd shears are vorpal blades indeed. And, while we are on the subject of blades, could Shakespeare have chosen a more shiversome name for an executioner than Abhorson?

ADMIRAL

ONE of the queerest things in word-history is that our English admirals should have come out of Arabia — or at least out of Arabic. The dictionaries make them Ameers or Emirs who have somehow become happily entangled with the classic admirable. So our chief naval commanders are, by origin, Praiseworthy Pashas. In view of this there was nothing strange about the attribution of admiralty to the more or less ancient Egyptians in Shakespeare's *Antony and Cleopatra*.

14

> Th' Antoniad, the Egyptian admiral,
> With all their sixty, fly, and turn the rudder;
> To see't mine eyes are blasted,

cries Enobarbus at Actium. To which Scarus replies

> Gods and goddesses,
> All the whole synod of them!

This yields a new collective noun for the Dark Blue Chiefs; synod has now become mainly ecclesiastical, but a Synod of Admirals is considerably more impressive than our dull-sounding Board. (After all Dr. Johnson could put a synod in the kitchen: 'Sir, we could not have had a better dinner, had there been a Synod of Cooks.')

Returning to the sea, let me confess that while I am, as a land-lubber, suitably impressed by Admirals and their works, I had never thought about their title or chased it into Araby, until I was set musing by some lines in an anonymous 'Plea for a Navy' (1436). The first stanza of this handsome prelude to our modern Navy League's counsel ends,

> Cheryshe marchandyse, kepe th' amyralté,
> That we bee maysteres of the narrow see.

Since that time admirals have been busily pacing the quarter-decks of our H.M.S. Parnassus, with Newbolt, Kiþling, and all the bold balladists proudly retorting to Cowper's

> Admirals, extolled for standing still
> Or doing nothing with a deal of skill.

Newbolt was especially devoted to home-sick sea-dogs, dying in a misty vision of combes and orchards, Lizard, Sound, and Hoe.

> Low on the field of his fame, past hope lay the
>   Admiral triumphant,
> And fain to rest him after all his pain.

That was the dying Blake, all Devon floating and gleaming in his consciousness.

Admirals, once Ameers or Emirs, are now among the Butterflies, Red Admiral the type, but not, of course, Russian. But for young men of the Navy they still apparently have Pasha-Status. Let me end with a brief war-story in confirmation. I had queued for and lawfully mounted a bus at rush-hour and found two young naval officers already aboard in high ecstasy. They pointed at the excellently neat, cheerful and unperturbed conductress who was keeping order over a mob of would-be passengers and telling some where they got off — or at least didn't get on. Cried one of the naval men in total bliss: 'She's just said, "You keep back, Old Cock" to an Air Vice-Marshal. Girlie, we'll bring you an Admiral to-morrow night.' The offer, as we have seen, was the sacrifice of no less than an Ameer.

ADORABLE

THERE is nothing novel or remarkable about this word, which has now been considerably diminished by over-use and misuse. Adore has descended from majestic heights in hymnal and liturgy to the swamp-music and galimatias of the cock-tail party. 'Oh my dear, too adorable', has been the measure of its ruin.

But adore and adorable give scope for some reflection on the emotional powers of the letter 'o'. This conveys, with its deep sonority, a certain nobleness. 'Glory to God' tunes fitly in with adoring. Again, descending from the celestial to the martial and the tribal, how much more inspiring as a war-cry is 'A Gordon, a Gordon' than 'A Stuart, a Stuart'. (Jews might rally more readily to inflict defeat upon a pogrom on hearing 'A Cohen, a Cohen' instead of 'A Levy, a Levy'.) Swinburne knew all about the value of the long 'o' followed by 'r' which gives to adoration a quality missing in the comparatively unimpressive word reverence. Tennyson no less. It is worth quoting the first verse of his brief poem 'Wages' to show what can be done with a sequence of 'o' syllables — and plenty of 'r's.

Glory of warrior, glory of orator, glory of song,
   Paid with a voice flying by to be lost on an endless sea —
Glory of Virtue, to fight, to struggle, to right the wrong —
   Nay, but she aim'd not at glory, no lover of glory she:
Give her the glory of going on, and still to be.

Returning to adorable, which should be properly and worship-fully employed, I must explain that I was inclined to these thoughts by some lines of Andrew Young on the Pilgrim's Way. Of St. Thomas and his shrine he wrote,

So I adored to-day
   No, not his ghost,
But the Saints in Westwell window
   And her the most
Who knelt there with no head
   But was so very
Adorable a Saint
   In a dress of crushed strawberry.

The measure and the rhymes, the conceit and the phrasing remind me of Humbert Wolfe, who was just the poet to use the word adorable with justice and respect in one of his own neat euphonies, so ingenious always in rhythm as in fancy.

ALDERLIEFEST

S A Y S Queen Margaret in *Henry VI*, Part 2, 'With you mine alderliefest sovereign'. Alder or aller is the old genitive plural of all: so alderliefest is dearest of all. The use of alder thus occurs nowhere else in Shakespeare, but it does occur among the works of Shakespeare's colleagues and rivals. Greene, for example, has

First, English King, I humbly do request
That by your means our princess may unite
Her love unto mine alderliefest love.

This does at least suggest another hand than William's in *Henry VI*, Part 2.

Lief as an adjective for dear is growing obsolete, but it survived thus in Tennyson's verse. More commonly it lives on, at least in poetry, as an adverb, meaning gladly or willingly.

> Could man be drunk for ever
> With liquor, love, and fights,
> Lief should I rouse at morning
> And lief lie down at nights.

Thus A. E. Housman, alderliefest singer to so many.

AMARANTH

THERE are some words which ring the bell wherever they are used. How many could immediately define the amaranth? Yet, in a line of verse, it brings with such swift ease all Arcady to mind. It is first the fadeless flower, a mythical bloom, then a purple blossom, perhaps a term for our love-lies-bleeding. Milton was prodigal of amaranth:

> Bid amaranthus all his beauty shed
> And daffadillies fill their cups with tears
> To strew the laureate hearse where Lycid lies.

It is the mourning and the grave-yard petal. Browning could rival Milton in this section of the floral dance:

> Whence the grieved and obscure waters slope
> Into a darkness quieted by hope;
> Plucker of amaranths, grown beneath God's eye
> In gracious twilights where His chosen lie.

Tennyson's Lotos-Eaters were 'propt on beds of amaranth and moly'. This poet played also with amaracus, the Cretan Dittany. (And Kipling, in turn, played in delight with dittany.) This from 'Œnone':

> Then to the bower they came;
> Naked they came to that smooth-swarded bower
> And at their feet the crocus brake like fire,
> Violet, amaracus, and asphodel,
> Lotos and lilies.

A bit too easy, no doubt, for the austere spasmodists of the nineteen-forties. But, like Bunthorne, I shall remain susceptible to amaranth and also to amaracus. No less I note that the prudent Walter de la Mare does not disdain the adjective amaranthine. And to Cowper, who thought of it as a synonym for immortal,

> The only amaranthine flower on earth
> Is virtue!

This links the word with lilies and languors, but for me it belongs to the rosy and the rapturous plantations, if roses can be undeciduous.

AMBUSCADE

OTHELLO'S ambuscadoes and our ambuscades have been mechanized by modern warfare into minefields and booby-traps, but they can still be true to their origin and be found in woodland. For the ambuscado, whose syllables seem to set cannon roaring in a Tudor tragedy, is the English form of the Italian imboscata. The ambush — poor-sounding child of ambuscado — is something which occurs in the boskage. But boskage could shelter as well as trap: hence the French *embusqué*. Ambuscades can still help the poet to give power to his line, where ambush would be of no avail. Dorothy Wellesley in her praise of 'Horses' imagines these old lures and traps that work in equine memory:

> Patient, adventuring still,
> A horse's ears bob on the distant hill,
> And he will start to hear
> A pheasant chuck or whirr, having the fear
> In him of ages filled with war and raid,
> Night-gallop, ambuscade.

It is the right final word, ending a stanza as decisively as it may end a life. In some lines of Edmund Blunden's it chimes in gravely and well.

> Sound not that long alarm, grey tower,
>   I know you well;
> This is your habit at this hour,
>   You and your bell!
> If once, I heard a hundred times
> Through evening's ambuscade your chimes,
>   Dark tower, your chimes.

'Evening's ambuscade' is a phrase of menace later made darker and more dangerous still by the gloom of war-time black-out.

AMETHYST

' QUARTZ coloured by manganese or by a compound of iron and soda.' Geology makes unromantic noises of this kind, but there is often mystery in the heart of it. 'The amethist staieth drunkennesse.' So thought the Tudor folk, who knew as much about drunkenness as most. The word, in its Greek derivation, makes this explicit claim. *A* — not, *methé* — intoxication. But what, having acquired a piece of quartz coloured by manganese, etc., did the toper do about it? Did he rest it on the aching brow or grind it to powder and swallow it at some risk to his duodenum? One suggestion, that wine drunk from an amethystine goblet would be a teetotal fluid, seems definitely to libel a blameless and beautiful stone.

Anyhow the colour of this quartz is violet-purple and so amethyst has been a jewel of esteem and amethystine an adjective appealing to many minor and some major poets. Dawns especially are amethystine and the epithet rides a sounding line as handsomely as frequently. The amethyst has Biblical honours and sounds the final note of celestial architecture and also of Mrs. Browning's 'Aurora Leigh'. (Does anybody cope with Aurora nowadays? It has imposing passages.)

> Where, faint and far,
> Along the tingling desert of the sky,
> Beyond the circle of the conscious hills,
> Were laid in jasper-stone as clear as glass
> The first foundations of that new, near Day
> Which should be builded out of heaven to God.

.   .   .   .

> 'Jasper first,' I said,
> 'And second, sapphire: third, chalcedony:
> The rest in order: last, an amethyst.'

The order, of course, is that in 'The Book of Revelation'. After chalcedony the chosen stones were emerald, sardonyx, sardius, chrysolite, beryl, topaz, chrysoprase, jacinth, and amethyst. Of the dozen the first two, jasper and sapphire, have acquired sinister significance in our giving of names. Sir Jasper in the melodramas was never anything but a sour, black-avised villain, scheming rape and ruin, and Sapphira's vice and fate have naturally discouraged wide usage of that stone at christenings. Beryl has been moderately popular and Sir Topaz we know at least in letters. Jacinth appears occasionally. But chalcedony, sardonyx, and chrysolite would be heavy birthday presents for any infant.

These minerals appear to have much in common. Chalcedony is 'a crypto-crystalline sub-species of quartz', transparent or translucent. In lapidary work it is called variously agate, cornelian, cat's eye, chrysoprase, onyx, sard. Agate is certainly a family name and Mr. Masefield has made Sard a Christian name, but not, I think, with minerals in mind. Amethyst has been very little used as a name for girls. It would be a classic and imposing alternative to Violet. It might become Ammy — but is that worse than Vi? If contracted to Misty it would have been very suitable for quite a number of scatterbrained young lovelies who never knew where they were lunching, with whom or when, but arrived at two instead of one, swathed in charm and faintly cooing 'Am I late?' War service, no doubt, has a little 'de-misted' them.

ANCILLARY and NOSTALGIC

Here is a word hard-pressed. The Latin ancilla was a hand-maiden; ancillae attended, for example, upon the deserted heroines whose griefs were sung by Ovid. Ancillary was naturally an adjective for subservient or subordinate. It was somehow absorbed into official English and 'ancillary services', for subordinate services, became common. It was odd that a maid from Roman boudoirs should so have wandered into the files of Whitehall. It was odder still, when ancillary was reduced to meaning merely additional and was used almost as an adverb. I have read sentences beginning 'Ancillary to this, the Committee suggests . . .' While we are on the subject of ancillary (and Ovid's heroines), why not reflect upon the fortunes of nostalgia and nostalgic? The Ovidian ladies undoubtedly suffered from nostalgia — the word meaning, by Greek derivation, an aching desire for a return to the old home. Was ever a term so overworked as nostalgia now? The offenders are not the officials this time, but the 'littery gents', who began to apply it without any reference to home or place. Because the word looked learned and imposing (as did ancillary) it was dragged in whenever possible. Anybody who wrote a book about the past with any sort of affection for bygone things was immediately and incessantly called nostalgic. You could hardly look at a page of book-reviews without seeing nostalgia and its epithet used (or misused) once or twice. Surely ancillary might now be released from official service and nostalgic restored to its proper, and topographical, significance.

AROMATIC

Pope has often been accused of failing in poetry, whatever tribute was paid to his brilliance in verse. Lytton Strachey defended him on this charge by quoting several lines. One was this, from 'An Essay on Man':

Die of a rose in aromatic pain.

Certainly here is music and bouquet too. The sonorous word 'aromatic', linked with the deep monosyllable 'rose' and the gently dolorous monosyllable 'pain', makes a beautifully balanced appeal to the senses. Strachey also quoted the adjacent description of the spider as being perfect in its natural observation and poetic phrase.

> The spider's touch, how exquisitely fine
> Feels at each thread and lives along the line.

I myself would add, from 'Windsor Forest', the description of the skylark's immortality which defies the fowler's gun.

> Oft, as the mounting larks their notes prepare,
> They fall, and leave their little lives in air.

The poet's sensibility could hardly be more poignant. But I am wandering from aromatic.

Aroma began as a spice and then was applied to any spicy or engaging odour. The noun, as it soars up to its long 'o' pitched between two short 'a's, has the form and splendour of a shapely arch. That quality accompanies the adjective. Use aromatic in any proper context and you have a pleasing iambic ready-made, if I may use that simple adjective instead of the more modish and more cumbrous Latinism of 'pre-fabricated'.

ATTERCOP

A LEADING authority on spiders, Dr. W. S. Bristowe, as well as some amateur entomologists, have reminded me that attercop has lingered long in the common speech, especially in Lancashire and east Scotland. There is so much in common between Danish and Scottish that attercop for spider seems natural in Fife, the Danish being Edderkopper. Attor or atter is the Old English for poison, and cop may be either head (kopf) or cup. Dr. Bristowe, who studies words as keenly as insects, likes 'a smother of spiders' as the noun of assembly when gossamer is in the making, explaining his choice thus:

> The spider population of an acre of grassland may be as much as 2,000,000. Under certain weather conditions, particularly warm sunny mornings in autumn, these spiders are stirred into uneasy wandering. They cover the grass stems, hedges and railings. Each trails a thread as they walk; so, in due course, the whole field may be covered with a shimmering silver sheet. I call this vast concourse 'a smother of spiders'. Gossamer is the result.

Gossamer, a word of flavour, is attributed to the time of year which Dr. Bristowe mentions, i.e. St. Martin's Summer, the Goose-summer. One of the best descriptions of a spider-smother morning is in Tennyson's 'In Memoriam', where there is a superb picture of an autumn day in the Wolds of Lincolnshire.

> Calm is the morn without a sound
>   Calm as to suit a calmer grief.
>   And only thro' the faded leaf
> The chestnut pattering to the ground:
>
> Calm and deep peace on this high wold,
>   And on these dews that drench the furze,
>   And all the silvery gossamers
> That twinkle into green and gold.

Dr. Bristowe adds:

> It is now too late to revive the ancient word tentbob (or taint-bob) in place of the clumsier and less descriptive harvester or harvest-mite, or to reintroduce such other attractive old English words as attercop (spider), pol-wiggle (tadpole) and oontie-tump (mole-hill), but one bids them good-bye with regret.

Tump is a word I much like. It suggests the dumping of a tumulus and has, in fact, often been applied to old grave-mounds. Hettie

Pegler's Tump is a famous Long Barrow. Our archaic tumps, often so finely shaped and nobly sited that they lie upon the summits like lions, look their best in gossamer weather. Then a smother of attercops works silken magic on these relics of the Ancient Mariners who spread their tracks and tombs across the chalky, flinty, downlands of the English coast. The dictionaries are silent about little Miss Muffet's tuffet, which I like to think is a rural diminutive of tump rather than a little tuft of vegetation, the former being a far likelier place for a whey-drinking session. It was undoubtedly a veritable attercop which so terrified Miss Muffet.

ATTRACTIVE

THERE is nothing particularly attractive about attractive: I mention it only to quote an R.A.F. correspondent who tells me that attractive in the 'officialese' of the Force means transportable. If that is at all general (he wrote from the Azores), it must be a curious archaism. Official English is usually vile and often seems to grow viler, but another correspondent gives a good mark to the Lords of the Admiralty for style as well as for manners. 'An example of this niceness', he writes, 'is the way in which Intend and Propose are used in the Navy. "Intend" means "I shall do this unless you tell me not to", while "Propose" means "I think it best to do this and do you agree?" The latter calls for an answer: the former does not.' Attractive usage, in the modern sense.

AUGMENT

IT surprised me to find, while reading *The Wonderful Old Gentleman*, one of the short stories of Miss Dorothy Parker,

> At five o'clock that afternoon the doctor had said that it would be a surprise to him if the Old Gentleman lasted till the middle of the night — a big surprise, he had augmented.

An English writer would have used added instead of augmented there. But the American keeps the old and modest English use of the word. Augmentation to Shakespeare was quite a humble matter. 'The new map with the augmentation of the Indies' means no more than with the addition of the Indies. But augment, with us, has now become imposing and formidable. It figures in 'commercialese' and showman's English. For example, in playbills announcing musical pieces, it is customary to announce 'A fully augmented chorus and orchestra' when extra players have been introduced. Just as in advertisements books are always profusely illustrated, so on the hoardings bands and choruses are always specially augmented. Nothing so common as enlargement or increase for them! But in America, it seems, augmenting can be still a minor matter.

AZURE AND CERULE

AZURE is another of our middle-eastern imports, Persia its home, lapis lazuli its nature. Hence a pigment and a colour. Chaucer used it of the jewel, 'a broche of golde and asure', but nowadays azure is nearly always the adjective for sky-blue. The 'z' makes it a little sticky on the tongue and therefore impedes the poet, but Sylvia Lynd, glorying in the 'unnecessary letter', has boldly used azure with zenith in a single line.

> I saw the sky at zenith clearest azure
> When white mists draw away at the sun's pleasure
> And at his golden touch the woods awaken.

Housman has azured as an adjective.

> Or littering far the fields of May
> Lady-smocks a-bleaching lay,
> And like a skylit water stood
> The bluebells in the azured wood.

Housman never fails in music, but 'azured wood' is a trifle harsh. G. M. Hopkins sings of 'grey-bells', azuring-over wood-banks and brakes in his 'May Magnificat'. It needs a Shakespeare to turn azure into music as well as colour. Of the sleeping Imogen Iachimo says,

> 'Tis her breathing that,
> Perfumes the chamber thus; the flame o' the taper
> Bows towards her; and would underpeep her lids
> To see the enclosed lights, now canopied
> Under these windows, white and azure, laced
> With blue of heaven's own tinct.

Heaven's own tinct. Azure is ever that. Phoebus is continually bidden to arise and paint the sable skies with azure. So commanded Drummond of Hawthornden who, master of the academic canvas and the Renaissance routine, never failed in a conventional richness. Skylarks have been vanishing into the azure for bardic centuries, but the word is never quite right for the job, lacking limpidity. It was a favourite of Francis Thompson's: he rhymed the 'z' with an 's' unfairly. Of the sun-god, pursuing Daphne, he wrote,

> Under the noon he made his prey sure
> Woofed in weeds of a woven azure.

Thompson, seeking for other blues, dragged in the Latin cerule, but it remains obstinately un-English.

> Ere eve has struck and furled
> The beamy-textured tent transpicuous
> Of webbed cerule wrought and woven colours.

This may be typical Thompson, but cerule does not help. Nor does it in his phrase 'sunken from thy cerule empery' applied to the setting sun.

BALCONY

O u r ancestors liked to lie snug: their windows, however noble the prospect, tended to be small. The warmer climates suggested larger lungs for the body of a house. We have drawn upon Italy for the balcony and upon Spain for the veranda. Balcony is a pleasing dactyl, romantic by nature and aptly named, too, for the bitter-sweet fun of such al fresco honeymooning as occurs in the first act of Noel Coward's *Private Lives*. Balcony has some kinship with our heavy English balk or beam, but how much lighter it is and how obviously planned for sleeping in the sun by day and listening to a serenade by night! Serenade is another of the good Latinities which arrived during the seventeenth century. (It was Serenate to Milton). These words were just too late for Shakespeare. All the world knows the Balcony Scene in *Romeo and Juliet*, but Shakespeare never thought of it so, for his vocabulary had no balconies, only galleries. To him and his fellows it was, presumably, the Orchard Scene. Serenade, for music, especially song, at night, is beyond improvement. It begins with 's', a letter which hisses tiresomely at times and is a source of pain to Mr. Clifford Bax, but it is his view that Tennyson's 'Tears, Idle Tears' might be deemed the most beautiful poem in the English language by a careful judge. (See p. 221 of his anthology with comments, *Vintage Verse*, a volume of brisk challenge as well as of abundant charm.) Yet 's' can hardly be fatal, for in this very poem of his delight there occurs,

> Ah, sad and strange as in dark summer dawns
> The earliest pipe of half-awaken'd birds
> To dying ears, when unto dying eyes
> The casement slowly grows a glimmering square:
> So sad, so strange, the days that are no more.

The first and the last two lines are full of 's'. Yet they are infinitely poignant. And remember Housman's

> I did not lose my heart in summer's even,
> When roses to the moonrise burst apart;

That is sibilant enough and yet it is glorious upon the lips.

Verandas, I think, are for a lounging romance and balconies for intrigues and serenades; casements, whether in Keats or Tennyson, lead simply to magic. Returning to the balcony, I have just found it applied to the female bosom, regarded as a site for jewels. Sir Osbert Sitwell, writing in *Left Hand, Right Hand!* of his great-

great-grandmother, Lady Conyngham, quotes Metternich's mistress Princess Lieven. 'Not an idea in her head; not a word to say for herself; nothing but a hand to accept pearls and diamonds with, and an enormous balcony to wear them on.' Sir Osbert does not accept this verdict. He rejects it, not from family pride, but because Lady Conyngham's relations with King George IV proved her to be no fool.

BARCAROLLE

THIS word has been commended to a wide British public by the justly favoured melody of Offenbach. Probably not all who esteem the air know that the title means a gondolier's song. It is certainly a perfect word for the romantic poesy of the shining night and the heart aglow. Public opinion has always accepted the moon as sentiment's proper, indeed inevitable, companion and why not a barcarolle to soothe the ear, as silvery beams entrance the eye? Tom Moore knew the trick of these dulcet things,

> When maidens sing sweet barcarolles,
>   And Echo sings again
> So sweet, that all with ears and souls
>   Should love and listen then.
> So, come to me when daylight sets:
>   Sweet! then come to me,
> When smoothly go our gondolets
>   Over the moonlit sea.

It is noticeable that he transfers his barcarolles from the watermen to the nymphs and takes the 'gondolets' (which have a tender, diminutive sound when compared with gondolas) from the canal to the sea. But would not a bard of to-day be justly scolded who rhymed 'then' with 'again'?

BASHAW

W E take our grandees from the East; naturally, since human grandeur is there itself most mammonlike and epicurean. The emir became the admiral. The Pasha became, for our eighteenth century, the Bashaw. Bashaws could be Indians or Anglo-Indian *nouveaux riches*, flaunting their rupees. 'The insolence of a Bashaw' continually resounds in the periods of Fielding and of the political pamphleteers of his century. If a Bashaw called up his game-keepers, bruisers, and cudgellers, or invoked what there was of law and order, to protect his property, his enemies still looking to the East, called them his Bashi-bazouks. Bashaws have now dropped out, but I have seen our police described by a strikers' defender as 'The Bashi-Bazouks in blue'. This was good journalism in the older, full-flown style. The Bashi-bazouks were irregular Turkish troops, notorious for brutal and licentious conduct. There is plainly something of powerful attraction in the word 'bash'. Why otherwise the lately developed Service habit of calling every kind of worker a basher, e.g. stores-basher, potato-basher, etc.? 'This word', says Eric Partridge in his *Dictionary of R.A.F. Slang*, 'is, in combination fast becoming man, chap, fellow.' It may be a sordid descent from old Bashaw to new Basher, but the word retains its fascination. To the R.A.F. no doubt, Eric Partridge is a word-basher, a title towards which I myself am working a modest passage.

BASILISK

T o basilisk, to fascinate, to conquer. This predecessor of our vulgar vamp, on which there is a note later on, I found in Surtees. His Mr. Rowley Rounding was a turnip-headed squire, hunting with the Heaviside. To him Facey Romford sold his lively horse Leotard. Leotard was to be ridden by Mrs. Rowley Rounding: but he was not underneath that dashing lady very long. (It needed

Mrs. Soapey Sponge to get the better of Leotard.) Mrs. Rounding had begun life as Brown ('Brown Stout' to the boys) and became Madame de Normanville. Madame, widowed, had an eye for men of acres, like Rounding, whom she met on Ramsgate Pier, where 'she basilisked the booby'. 'Next day she had him as handy as a French poodle and looking about as sensible. And widows, being generally pretty good men of business, short, sharp, and decisive, she brought him to the "what have you got and what will you do?" gate without giving him a chance of leading her over it.' Such was basiliskery.

The original basilisk was a reptile, begotten of a cock and a serpent, complete with barbed tail. Its other name was cockatrice. It suffered seriously from halitosis and its best friends would shrink apprehensively away: its enemies were either withered at a glance or overwhelmed with a breath. It could be as fatal as any blood-sucking vampire. Basilisks were cannon as well as monsters to Shakespeare and Marlowe. As such they roared and shook down turrets. But Shakespeare has the other basilisk too. When Posthumus is given Imogen's bracelet by Iachimo as proof of her infidelity, he cries,

> It is a basilisk unto mine eye,
> Kills me to look on't.

Basilisk, as well as vampire, came down in the world. But to basilisk a gentleman, instead of vamping him, is certainly a word which blondes of taste might well prefer.

The poet Cornelius Whurr, of whom I know little save that he was born a hundred years ago (1845), has imperishably remarked,

> What lasting joys that man attend
> Who has a polished female friend!

I am sure that such a companion would never have vamped Cornelius, but she might have gone so far as to attempt a little intellectual basiliskery with well-chosen quotations from the more amorous of the classical poets.

31

BATLING

I N a previous volume Batling appeared as a seventeenth-century fish in the company of Peele and Tweete, swirling handsomely down the stream of John Dennys's piscatorial verses. But batling (or battling) is also an adjective for fertile or fertilized. Robert Greene once wrote:

> these Oxford schooles
> Are richly seated neere the river side:
> The mountaines full of fat and fallow deere,
> The batling pastures laid with kine and flocks,
> The towne gorgeous with high built colledges,
> And schollers seemely in their grave attire,
> Learned in searching principles of art.

To describe Headington and Boar's Hill as mountains seems the mark of an impressionable man, but the rest of the description is right as well as complimentary. It is odd that Greene should have used batling of the water-meadows round the very city where the verb to battel or battle, for nourish, has principally survived. The Oxford undergraduate's battels are his nourishment and the bill therefore. The College kitchen, as well as the neighbouring farms, are places of batling.

BELVEDERE AND GAZEBO

B E L V E D E R E, meaning a room (or even a rock) with a view, is not commonly used. I was happy to find this formal, Italianate term in Mr. W. A. Poucher's *Escape to the Hills*. Mr. Poucher is an expert photographer, and he must be a man of infinite patience as well as of rare agility in order to obtain his clear, cloudless views of our so often sodden and bemisted peaks. Belvedere is a favourite word of his for the right niche to stop at in order to look and to wonder. His use of belvedere is certainly justified by the pictures that he collects. 'Hall's Fell Tap', he writes of Saddleback, 'is an admirable belvedere', and I have enjoyed on the spot fairly recent confirmation of this opinion. But belvederes have really more smack of the Renaissance than of Cumbrian crags and refer, as a rule, to turrets or to windowed rooms specially designed for those whose tranquil pleasure is to sit and stare when their fortune is to be in pleasant places. I met, in print, a Belvedere of this kind when, realizing that I have never attempted Browning's 'Red Cotton Nightcap Country', I set to work on it.

> And now the tower a-top I took for clock's
> Or bell's abode, turns out a quaint device,
> Pillared and temple-treated Belvedere —
> Prevailing safe within its railed-about
> Sublimity of area — whence what stretch
> Of sea and land, throughout the seasons' change
> Must greet the solitary.

A full definition.

Gazebo (three syllables with the 'e' long) is the same article as a Belvedere. There are two theories of its origin. One is that Gazebo is a jesting alternative to the Latin *Videbo* — I shall see. The other assumes a corruption of some Oriental word, because the earlier uses of Gazebo associate it with Eastern oddities. Where the scholars disagree I shall modestly withdraw, surmising that Gazebo is perhaps better applied to such an alien-spirited niche as the Pagoda summit in Kew Gardens, while Belvedere is kept for classic architecture. What then of Nature itself? One most exquisite place of this kind in my acquaintance is a shelter built of rock, with ample windows. Contrived upon the coast of the Isle of Jura it looks south to the Paps and east to the coast of Argyll: behind that and sweeping away to the north-east is the huge tumble of the Western Highlands from Lomond to Glencoe.

Behind the walls and windows are a peat fire, and, among other books, the complete works of R. L. Stevenson. Belvedere-gazebo indeed!

BLINKING

T H E following comment on my note on the adjective blinking in a previous volume has been sent to me by a colleague in journalism, Mr. Anthony Hern: —

I think you will find that words like blinking owe nothing to Shakespeare but everything to prudery, particularly the public prudery of the industrial age. Blinking, like blasted and blurry, are shunt-words from the objectionable adjective bloody. If ever you get around to writing a third word-book, I hope you may be able to devote a little space to these shuntings. They are at once proof of versatility in coining and of comment on morals. Darned, dashed were speedy substitutes for damned — on which the ghosts of Bowdler placed their sealed-lips veto for many years. At a time when the word in print was usually conveyed by a long metal rule or by d——d, Baroness Orczy managed to break the barrier by referring to the 'demm'd elusive Pimpernel', thus giving to the dreaded word a salving flavour of aristocracy. *Très snob*, in fact! Perhaps the commonest shunted formations are those which stem from the now-almost-forgotten laws against blasphemy — exclamations like gosh and golly, cripes and crumbs, though words sent up a siding from the main line of oaths calling on God and Christ, were yet admitted, in presumably blissful ignorance, into the so-pure pages of writers of stories about pseudo-public school life like Warren Bell and others whose names now are as though blacked-out by ink-daubs. Once 'classy' epithets like By Jove and By Jupiter were not evidence of classical erudition or a heathenish disposition: they too had been neatly shunted away from the once-common invocation to Jesus. Not all such shuntings have received form-room blessing. 'For crying out loud', a rather clumsy and Americanized 'shunt' from 'For Christ's sake' is still looked upon as rough and unpleasant by people to whom 'By Jiminy' sounds merely quaint.

There is abundant exercise to be had in tracing the 'shunt-words' employed for the various bodily functions held to be unmentionable. In the midst of these researches and reflections one inevitably notes the fact that the letter 'b' is our favourite token of dismissal, That the labial effort used in pronouncing it is a kind of spitting is one obvious explanation. At any rate the two commonest impolite words for a disliked man and woman both begin with 'b', and it is doubtful whether bastard would have become (so unjustly) a term of abuse if it had begun with another letter. Dastard, for example, has almost dropped out, but bastard (with shunt-word basket) is very frequently heard. 'Bl' is a particularly common beginning for terms of disgust. Fools are blasted, blighted, blinking, blithering and blistering, as well as blatant, blooming and bloody. Blimey is an obscure expletive assisted by that 'bl' opening. And why is anybody a bloke? Bloke has found its way to literature and dictionary honours, but even the O.E.D. cannot explain its origin.

BORBORYGMY

WRITING on 'Poetry in Scotland' recently Mr. Hugh Macdiarmid alluded to the

> immense 'dish o' whummle' — this vast wind-pie — upon which successive generations of Scots have been 'nourished' to the exclusion of their proper pabulum. No wonder the result has been an Anglo-Scottish literature of little but flatulence and borborygmy.

Whummle I could, as a Scot, place. It is, I believe, confusion. But borborygmy? As a one-time classic I should have been able to define this imposing Grecian, but was driven to the dictionary. It appears to be a rumbling in the bowels and for that sounds gastrically right. (The word is much rarer than the ailment.) Hence comes borborology for the rumblings of unclean talk and one expects an adjective borborygmatous for rumblers. 'The profound silence of Fogeys' Club after luncheon was disturbed only by the occasionally audible distress of borborygmatous old men.' But the epithet has no authority save my own. On the other hand there is Borborite, 'One of the names or nick-names given to certain Ophitic Gnostics, according to Epiphanius, because of their unclean living' and so applied in the sixteenth and seventeenth centuries to any holder of filthy opinions or bestial doctrine. Ignorance of the Ophitic Gnostics and their nasty habits need not bar us from use of the word. To call your opponent a Borborite would certainly be a relief. This is the kind of term much affected in his early days by Aldous Huxley who loved a long Grecian noise, especially for physical matters. Surely he must somewhere have written of Steatopygous (broad-based) victims of incessant borborygmy.

CAPUCHIN

THE capuchin was something for the caput, a hood or the sharp-pointed headdress worn by the Franciscan friars who were called capuchins accordingly. It then became a woman's cloak and hood combined and as such appears in the Scottish ballad of Mally Lee, 'extracted and slightly altered (by Robert Chambers) from a manuscript collection written by a lady of rank, since 1760'.

> As Mally Lee came down the street,
>   Her capuchin did flee;
> She coost a look behind her
>   To see her negligee.

Mally had 'two lappels at her head, that flaunted gallantlie', also 'a genty shape' and naturally took the eye of all the beaux in Canongate. But she was proud and disdainful, as is the way with such parties in ballads. Capuchin was later applied to black-haired monkeys and black-plumed pigeons whose heads suggested the wearing of a cowl.

CARESS

I T is queer that this gently sensual, sweetly insinuating word should have been known to the author of *Paradise Lost* but not to the singer of Romeo and Antony, Juliet and Cleopatra. The liquid second syllable of this seventeenth-century derivation from the Italian *carezza* pours melody into many a line. Listen to it in A.E.'s lullaby strain.

> Dusk wraps the village in its dim caress;
> Each chimney's vapour, like a thin grey rod,
> Mounting aloft, through miles of quietness,
> Pillars the skies of God.

These lines are as striking in their softness as are Shakespeare's 'black vesper's pageants' in their severity. A.E. had some favourite words which he seemed to overwork; at least that is the impression you get from taking his mysticism *en masse*. Dim and glimmering are constant with him.

> The dim and silver end of day
> Scarce glimmered through the little room

is typical A.E. and how rich in faint light is that first line! More strangely, diamond and diadem are frequently recurrent. The last is awkward-sounding and not, to me, an attractive word. Day, night, and winter are all diamond to him.

> Its edges foam'd with amethyst and rose,
> Withers once more the old blue flower of day:
> There, where the ether like a diamond glows,
> Its petals fade away.

A.E.'s way with words was a caress.

CARGOZOON

M A N Y of our Spanish and Italian importations have been be-littled as they passed the docks. How much more impressive was lemonado than lemonade! This latter came in during the middle of the seventeenth century. Bringing the Cargazon or Cargozoon to English harbours, we made it cargo, a good word and conveniently brief, but far less satisfying to a man with a taste for sounding terms. Cargozoons were still afloat in the seventeenth century. In the Epilogue to the comedy of *Sir Courtly Nice*, we read,

> Another waits above in the great Room
> Till a new Cargozoon of Strumpets come.

Here the word is formidable indeed as a noun of improper assembly.

CHOAS

J U S T a mistake, but interesting. A paper, of a somewhat Fiery and Forward type, came to my office. It was called *The Irish Democrat*, New Series, Number One. The first streamer headline of New Series, Number One, ran 'End the Travel Choas'. This I liked. It put up a formidable rival to the O'Casey Paycock's 'Terrible State of Chassis'. Moreover, the choas in the printer's office gave some powerful support to the common error of so many highly educated people who use the word 'inchoate' as though it were 'inchaote' and meant chaotic. Inchoate, as I repeat from time to time, means 'only just begun, rudimentary', whereas it is commonly applied to what is overthrown and confused. Choas, accordingly, would be a nice short word for the state of inchoation, certainly briefer and more vivid than rudimentariness.

CICISBEO

A LADY's man, an Italianate gallant or lover of married women, a beaugarzoon, as the Restoration dramatists would have called him. The epithets for the type are as interesting as the noun. A cicisbeo, in the world of Shadwell and his colleagues, could be shanty or ganty. Both mean sparkish.

CLARET

NOT a striking word, yet obviously it has its appeal. Why otherwise should it have usurped, as far as Britain is concerned, the red wines of Bordeaux? It signifies clear wine, but claret is not markedly clear. The victory is an odd one. Dr. Johnson's absurdly crude view that claret is a wine for boys, with port allotted to men, was never shared in Scotland. I like the lines of Allan Ramsay after he has surveyed the snow on 'Pentland's tow'ring tap' and called for the 'tappit hen' which is a Scots quart stout-stoop or English half-gallon.

> Good Claret best keeps out the Cauld
> And drives away the Winter soon,
> It makes a Man baith gash and bauld,
> And heaves his Saul beyond the Moon.

This proper attribution to claret of brave, spirit-lifting and trans-lunar powers preceded Johnson's nonsense in time and answered it before it was spoken.

Gash is sagacious. A man with a long chin the Scots used to call 'gash gabbet'. I must remember that when next I have the pleasure of reviewing a Jack Hulbert show. Has Hulbert ever, when delighting Glasgow or Edinburgh, found himself described as gash gabbet in *The Glasgow Herald* or *The Scotsman*? Probably not. Scots journalists are proud of their English (justly) and their readers have mainly ceased to understand Scots. I read that gash has now become a naval term for anything free or 'scrounged'.

But we are wandering from the pleasures of claret, a term adjectively applied by Herrick to the cheeks of a charmer. Most of the clarets we drank of late (and hope to drink again) are not of a colour with which ladies would like to be much imbued. Andrew Young, on the other hand, writes of the 'claret-coloured briches', when describing a Highland glen in winter. He thus gives support to my previous contention that wine-dark, seemingly wrong for the Aegean seas on whose surface Greek epic spawned it, will do very well for the bloom coming off our native woods in winter. I certainly know combes, denes and bottoms in the English shires where a vapour, hanging over the leafless twigs upon a sun-shot winter afternoon, is fairly to be described in terms of the Bordeaux vintages. The sight of it is so exquisite as to heave one's soul, if not beyond the moon, at least slightly over one's shoulders.

It is queer that the British should call two such important wines as Bordeaux and Rhenish by names strange to the growers. Claret was a word used in Elizabeth's England. It occurs once in Shakespeare, if you permit *Henry VI*, Part 2 to be Shakespeare's own. Jack Cade, when enjoying his brief triumph in rebellion, proclaims claret now to be everyman's tipple, though he puts it more grossly. Hock began to edge its way in early in the following century. Hamlet speaks of Rhenish and Shakespeare uses the term several times. The victory of Hock is surprising; it is an abbreviation of Hockamore, an Anglicization of Hochheimer. Hochheim is on the Main, not the Rhine. But it was important enough to give a general name in England to the Rhine wines as well as to its own.

COFFIN

COFFIN to the Elizabethan was any kind of coffer or container: it was commonly used for a pie-dish or even a pie-crust. Shakespeare's Titus Andronicus (if he was Shakespeare's), when gnashing his teeth and turning up his sleeves for barbaric vengeance and nasty work in the kitchen, cried:

Hark, villains! I will grind your bones to dust,
And with your blood and it I'll make a paste,
And of the paste a coffin I will rear
And make two pasties of your shameful heads.

Coffin for pie-dish I found in a gruesome passage of Gervase Markham's *The English Hus-wife* (1623). It reminded me that I was once bidden to a lunch at which the dishes were all to be concocted according to Tudor recipes. The fish and meat, both of which might have been excellent in their natural state, were swamped in all manner of spices and even fruits and thus rendered so rich as to be nauseous. Readers of Markham will sympathize with my queasy response to this old-world hospitality, for here is his counsel on the handling of a leg of mutton.

> Take a leg of mutton, and cut the best of the best flesh from the bone, and parboil it well; then put to it three pound of the best mutton suet, and shred it very small: then spread it abroad, and season it with pepper and salt, cloves and mace: then put in good store of currants, great raisins and prunes, clean washed and picked, a few dates sliced, and some orange pills sliced: then being all well mixed together, put it into a coffin, or into divers coffins and so bake them: and when they are served up, open the lids, and strew store of sugar on the top of the meat, and upon the lid. An in this sort you may also bake beef or veal; only the beef would not be parboiled, and the veal will ask a double quantity of suet.

Is it surprising that, with their culinary coffins so packed, the Tudor folk expected to reach the other kind of coffin a good deal earlier than we do? To put six pounds of suet to three of veal and then to get busy with the cloves, raisins, prunes, and sugar! Small wonder too that the Elizabethans were obviously prone to halitosis and 'B.O.' and liked to have scent sprayed in the rooms where there was much company. The physician Boorde, writing in the previous century, had warned his public of evil vapours in the bedroom, adding that 'the breath of man may putrify the air within the chamber'. After a good dollop of veal coffined with these suety trimmings this might well occur.

COSSET AND TANTONY

C O S S E T was a noun before it was a verb. It was the pet lamb, the shepherd's favourite in the flock, and so any loved one. As moppet, a little fish, became a little darling (human and feminine) so cosset became the sweet and spoiled one. And then, for some reason, it was forgotten as a noun and kept alive as a verb. People now cosset anything, not fair ones only, but their children, their health, their whims. We have moved a long way from the usage of Stephens, the Jacobean essayist, who liked to see his 'cosset wanton', i.e. his pet lamb frisk. (See later note on Mithridate.)

Tantonies were in the pig-sty what cossets were in the sheep-fold. Since St. Antony was the patron of the Swine-herds and was often pictured with a pigling in attendance, the tantony became a name for the smallest of a sow's litter. It was then employed as a symbol of faithful or obsequious following. The verb to tantony, i.e. to fawn, was next introduced, like Shakespeare's 'To spaniel'. Tantony was rarely, if ever, a term of genuine affection, like cosset, and sometimes both were used in a depreciatory manner. The O.E.D. gives an instance of the two words in company. 'Some are such Cossets and Tantonies that they congratulate their Oppressors and flatter their Destroyers' (1659). It is odd that tantony never became a synonym for darling, for it is a darrlin' word, as Sean O'Casey's Joxer Daly would have said. If men could turn a moppet (little fish) into a term of affection, why not tantony, for little pigs are easy conquerors of the human heart?

COTQUEAN

COTQUEAN occurs in that queer, not obviously needed, little scene of *Romeo and Juliet* (iv. 4) in which Capulet is hurrying on the preparations for the marriage-feast. The Nurse, with her usual frankness, bids him keep clear of larder and pantry matters. 'Go, you cotquean, go,' she commands. A cotquean, for her, was a man who busies himself with women's affairs. Why? The word meant originally a cottage woman, therefore a rough-and-ready house-wife. So a masculine hand at work on feminine concerns suggested a conversion of the term and Restoration comedy bandies cotquean as a term of mockery. Addison, who would have been no admirer of the feminine M.P., wrote: 'A stateswoman is as ridiculous a creature as a cotquean: each of the sexes should keep within its bounds.' The husband who must show his hand as a cook (usually less enthusiastic when there is need for the hand of the scullery-maid in washing-up) is the cotquean of to-day. Jonson used the resonant noun cotqueanity.

CRACK

THERE can be few words of more various meaning than crack and the present popularity of 'get cracking' as an incitement to almost any kind of activity shows that crack is still a favourite. Crack in Shakespeare is a gay urchin as well as that rending and menacing noise, the crack of doom. As a brisk child crack does, I think, survive in some pastoral English. Thieves have long had crack in their cant for house-breaking. We need not bother about crack's conventional use for a blow. More interesting is its employ-ment for forms of talk, usually exaggerated, lurid gossip-talk. That links us up with the modern wise-crack, a word which would have been understood more easily by a man of the eighteenth than of the nineteenth century. A crack was also the maker of such conversa-tional cracks and Addison used it, perhaps by mistake, for a crank.

The same writer linked 'cracking and boasting'. Crack as an adjective for first-rate is hard to explain. It has worked its way up from slang, but is now orthodox, especially when applied to military and athletic matters. Regiments and marksmen are often crack. People are cracks at games, but not at the arts. Are there crack sopranos and ballet-dancers? Both classes might well resent the epithet, since cracking is a process which befalls voices and joints to the disadvantage of the owners.

CRASSITUDE

HAVING previously mentioned Housman's hebitude as a good bludgeon of a word for the battering of a thick skull, I feel that crassitude deserves almost equal honour and employment. The word has further relevance to a previous note of mine since it was linked by Carlyle, as several correspondents have reminded me, with the adjective inspissated. I had commented on the fact that inspissated was an epithet now only (and with sickening monotony) applied to gloom. It was, I have since discovered, Dr. Johnson who launched inspissated gloom upon our speech and the grandeur of the first of these words has turned his creation into a cliché. We could rescue inspissation by following Carlyle's example and occasionally hurling 'the inspissated crassitude of the Opposition' across the floor of the House or likewise dismissing into the depths of hebetic ignominy the author of a book or play which strikes us as dull folly. Again, crassitude might become a form of decoration. 'On retirement from office he was given the Order of Crassitude, First class, Inspissated, and died in peaceable enjoyment of the same.'

CROON

CROON has come to mean a melancholy moaning, apparently holding for its fanciers some anodyne or even positively aphrodisiac qualities. It began life as a verb of tremendous and thunderous application. The first meaning of croon in O.E.D. is 'to utter a continued, loud, deep sound: to bellow as a bull, roar, low; to boom as a bell'. The lordly bull in a poem of Southey's croons to the hills which in turn recroon the roar. With the passage of years the word grows steadily gentler and descends from a roar to a lamentation and then, more especially, to a low murmuring of song. Still, it could be associated with true masculine types. Burns's Tam o'Shanter was a crooner.

> Tam skelpit on thro' dub and mire
> Despising wind, an' rain, an' fire,
> Whiles holding fast his gude blue bonnet,
> Whiles crooning o'er some auld Scots sonnet.

Browning discovered crooning in the fiddler's art. His violin parade in 'Red Cotton Nightcap Country' ends with,

> Over this sample would Corelli croon
> Grieving, by minors, like the cushat dove,
>   Most dulcet Giga, dreamiest Saraband.
> From this did Paganini draw the fierce
> Electric sparks or to tenuity
> Pull forth the inmost wailing of the wire:
> No cat-gut could swoon out so much of soul.

(Corelli was a maestro of the late seventeenth century, Giga his jig.)
    The last line carries us on to the crooning of the immediate hour. 'Swooning out of soul' might, unless you are jealous for the word soul, be applied to the modern moan.

> We'll meet again,
> Dunno where, dunno when!

What a tearful, husky boo-hoo-hoo it is! So at last, from the farmers' paddock or banks of Doon, the word has meandered to Hollywood and our music-hall microphones. Mr. Crosby croons to conquer: so do Miss Vera Lynn, Miss Ann Shelton, and Mr. Frank Sinatra. The latter, whose croonery has so powerfully pixilated American womanhood, is not, I gather, of a taurine vigour nor would he make the mountain-tops recroon his melody. However, one thing is certain. The word croon was never more widely on the lips of men and women than in an age whose real motto is, 'Let the people listen'. It is in essence a fine word, but it has been turned to odd usage. The habits of the modern crooner always strike me as wildly paradoxical; the sentiments that used to make the bosom swell, the heart beat, and the eyes shine, the joys of reunion, of moonlit courtship, of discovering port after stormy seas, and so on, seemingly reduce him or her to the most profound abysms of melancholy. And the sadder grows the singer (if that is not too complimentary a word) the happier do the million listeners become amid their mush of lachrymose felicity.

CURMUDGEON AND MECANTODOR

ACCORDING to an anonymous correspondent of Dr. Johnson's, curmudgeon is a Scottish term, created by the Scottish habit of appropriating and telescoping the French phrases, with which the Old Alliance had made people familiar. (Gardyloo for gardez l'eau is the common example.) Curmudgeon, on this model, is coeur méchant. This explanation is not generally accepted, but there is an interesting parallel. I have been told that old leases of houses, in the east of Scotland, used to guarantee the purchaser or tenant against mecantodor, this being méchant odeur. But I have never had confirmation of this from a lawyer. At any rate it is nice to believe that satisfactory plumbing once led to so handsome a title. Leading articles about housing (and lawyers' leases too) would be far easier reading if they were aflame with such Norman decoration as this. Indeed, a Sonnet of Real Estate could properly soar to some such concluding line as

A Messuage without Mecantodor.

DAYLIGONE

A N Ulster correspondent kindly sent me this word (short for 'daylight-gone') as a local usage for twilight or eventide. It is certainly a nice one and it seems that it has found its way into print in Lynn Doyle's *Ballads of Ballygullion*. It is not a dictionary word, but investigating the lexicon led to the discovery that English words for daybreak have indeed been many and charming. Over and above day-break and day-dawn, there are day-peep, day-rawe, day-red, and day-rim. More abiding has been the day-spring, which the Church of England has preserved in Tindale's phrase about our visitation by 'the day-spring from on high'. Milton had it too, showing 'the breath of heaven' to be fresh-blowing and 'with day-spring born'. From dayspring to dayligone suggests long, basking hours in a warm and lucid air.

DECUMAN AND DECIBEL

T H A T unflagging Latinist, Francis Thompson, wrote of

The lover whose soul shaken is
In some decuman billow of bliss.

The decuman is the tenth or largest wave and the word has accordingly been used to express unusual size or strength. Decibel, presumably a tenth of something, has been recently used as a unit of sound. It is an attractive word, but one finds it applied rather to the more odious clangours and screechings of modern life than to

47

sweetness of music or song. It is the thudding, mechanic, road-ripping drill and not the nightingale that is considered in terms of decibels. So, when tanks are 'sounding through the town' with grimmer justification for that splendid verb than was ever provided by the bonnie Earl of Moray, one thinks of a new participle, decibelligerent. One can fit the almost delicate word decibel into many agreeable rhythms and metres. However, it must be reserved mainly for tumult and braying and clatter of all kinds. A Muscovite victory-salvo, for example, might be compiled in terms of decibellic output and described as a veritable decuman of din.

DELIQUIUM

S w o o n , or swound, is a good word for its subject. But, if you are feeling classically inclined and want to pass out, if not away, in a grave, Augustan style, why not consider the attraction of deliquium? It is true that I found it (in Miss Dorothy Stuart's *Regency Roundabout*) applied to a fatal swoon, but it need not always be so serious. Here is the narrative, quoted by Miss Stuart concerning 'the truly respectable Widow Neale'. The widow was a pew-rent collector, who, though fatigued, went faithfully in search of these ecclesiastical dues in the neighbourhood of Church Street, Kensington. 'At Kensington Gore her strength failed her, her spirits flagged, and she sank down upon the footpath in the deliquium of death. And mark we the boasted humanity of the spot! Her silken umbrella was stolen from a faint and lifeless grasp: she was refused admission to the next public house . . .' Ultimately she was recognized, put into a coach, and died on the journey home. Such was Regency Kensington. Not even a small brandy for the moribund. We had thought more kindly of those liquorish times. But, as I said, deliquia could be much less severe and more akin to a minor visitation of the vapours. Did Gibbon ever use deliquium of the declining Roman Empire? He might well have done. The word has the sonority, rhythm, and flavour of his style.

DISEMBOGUE

T H I S massive word for outflow was used by Pope to describe the famous ditch by whose vanished banks I happen to be writing. I have heard that, though the foul Fleet Ditch, famed for a thousand stenches, has long been reduced to a decent drain, the taximen have inherited the term for a cabstand hereabout and still talk of 'The Ditch'. Here are Pope's lines:

> This labour past, by Bridewell all descend,
> (As morning-pray'r and flagellation end)
> To where Fleet-ditch with disemboguing streams
> Rolls the large tribute of dead dogs to Thames,
> The King of Dykes! Than whom no sluice of mud
> With deeper sable blots the silver flood.

Disemboguing seems exactly right for so horrid a runnel. Southey, however, used it of fair streams and limpid waters. The verb originally meant to emerge from the mouth of a stream and was applied to ships getting to sea. But then it was transferred to the stream itself or to any eruptive object.

> Volcanoes bellow ere they disembogue,

was one of Young's Night Thoughts. Disembogue could be transitive too. The old Irish nurse's fearful menace of 'I'll tear the tripes out of you' (really uttered with no sort of unkindly or surgical intention) might have been spoken by her Tudor ancestress, 'I'll disembogue your innards'. But disembogue is best as Pope used it, especially for some Acheron of an industrial town, darkly oozing on its way. Manchester's Irwell surely disembogues.

DIZEN

D I Z E N for dress or trick out has faded away since the eighteenth
century. It has survived in bedizen, whose 'be' is really unnecessary,
for to speak of a bedizened hussy is no more rude than to denounce
a dizened one, as Goldsmith would have called the lady. According
to Synge's Pegeen Mike, the mother of the Pharaoh was such an
one. 'I'm thinking you're too fine for the like of me, Shawn Keogh
of Killakeen, and let you go off till you'd find a radiant lady with
droves of bullocks on the plains of Meath, and herself bedizened in
the diamond jewelleries of Pharaoh's ma.' Ma is superb. It so
thoroughly puts the Ancient Dynasts in Michael Flaherty's bar.

DIZZARD

I N a catalogue of abuse Burton's dizzard comes aptly in. It means
a dizzy-witted man, blockhead or feckless fellow.

> How would our Democritus have been affected, to see a
> wicked caitiff or fool, a monster of men, a dizzard, a covetous
> wretch, a beast, a filthy loathsome carcass, assume unto himself
> glorious titles! To see another neat in clothes, spruce, full of
> courtesy, empty of grace and wit, talk nonsense! To see so many
> lawyers, so little justice; the judge bribed, sentence prolonged.
> What's the world itself? A vast chaos, the theatre of hypocrisy,
> a shop of knavery.

The passage has something, but by no means all, of Hamlet's phrasing and philosophy. These picturesque lamentations upon villainy
are common to all ages, but the Tudor and Jacobean men had
especially the trick of it, whether they were laying on their bastinado
to the dizzards or the daughters of the game.

DOWLY

A FRIEND of mine from the North-East coast calls a dull day a dowly day. What an excellent word, containing the very genius of a heavy, scowling melancholy! Dowly should be widely used of people as well as of skies. It is too expressive to be limited in scope or left to dialect. Dowly times were 'dirk and drublie' to Dunbar, whose

> In to thir dirk and drublie dayis
> Quhone sabill all the hevin arrayis
> With mystie vapouris, cluddis, and skyis
> Nature all curage me denyis
> Off sangis, ballatis, and playis,

strikes into the very heart of a modern Scottish Sabbath in December. For such a murk on Clydeside the adjective dowly seems almost inadequate.

DRAPED AND DRUNKULENT

D R A P E D , as an epithet for tipsy, is a piece of war-time slang that has restored a slight element of fancy and poetry to the exhilaration conferred by Dionysos. A man is draped who hangs on to the palings or his companions, so that drapery may be considered to signify a fairly advanced stage of alcoholic collapse. But how much better it is than the wearisome, unimaginative words so often selected by the English for this condition! Perhaps it is realistic, but it is also dull, to say of a man that he is blind, oiled, blotto, soaked, swamped, bottled, or canned. Draped is a more gracious metaphor. Tipsy, with its suggestion of tottering, hints at the condition immediately precedent to drapery. Music-hall comedians in their Drunken Swell turns continually pass from the tipsy motion to the draped posture. It is a pity that tipsy, which is Shakespearean and Miltonic, and has some age and bouquet, should have been passed over to the genteel lingo of maiden aunts. No man would now ask another whether he was tipsy last night. The word is too spinsterish. Perhaps *draped* will spread. It should. It has descriptive pungency. An old usage, which seems to have wholly vanished, is that of *disguised* for drunk. This occurs with some frequency in Restoration comedy. Dr. Johnson's Dictionary gives, 'Disguise. Disorder by drink'.

Drunkulent is a joke and a portmanteau. But surely good of its kind. Indeed, *drunkulent* seems to me admirably expressive for one who is pugnaciously 'lit-up'. It would be a nice addition to our police-court lingo. 'The prisoner approached me in a drunkulent manner.' Or, in less rough society, 'You seem a little drunkulent this evening' might be heard on the fringe of a cocktail party after some interchange of argument. Such a challenge might evoke from its recipient a repetition of the immortal protest, 'I'm not so think as you drunk I am!'

DRINK, THE

I T is common knowledge that 'the dickens' (for the devil) is as old as Shakespeare. 'I cannot tell what the dickens his name is', says Mistress Page. It is less well known how much of our modern slang is as old as Dickens. The catch phrase of a generation ago, 'Yes, I don't think' is at least as ancient as the Weller family and a correspondent has just reminded me that some of the Air Force slang of to-day was in use a century ago. An example of these phrases, born far-away and long ago and yet surviving, is to be found in the usage of 'the drink' for the sea or a wide river. This occurs in *Martin Chuzzlewit*, chapter 23. The passage runs as follows:

> An instance of neglect which caused the 'Capting' of the *Esau Slodge* to wish he might be sifted fine as flour and whittled small as chips, that if they didn't come off that there fixing right smart too, he'd spill 'em in the drink, whereby the Capting metaphorically said he'd throw them in the river.

It is a striking reminder of the continuity of slang. For the 'Capting' of the *Esau Slodge* was, of course, an American: presumably the phrase had been brought across 'the drink' from England.

Rules are there to be broken. So, having decided not to rifle, as yet, the treasury of place-names, I am making exception of Elsinore. I had thought — and many, surely, must have shared my opinion — that Shakespeare's *Hamlet* had been abundantly enriched in its music by this sounding and seductive name. But it is not so. On referring to the Concordance I found that Elsinore is mentioned only four times and never after the second Act. Queer, for I would have sworn that the whole play rang with it.

Of Elsinore I can fairly write with affection, having been there several times, always with pleasure. During one visit the English Players were in Elsinore, playing *Hamlet* in the castle known as Kronborg. On another occasion the Danish Players were in the town, offering a Revy (revue) called *Tempo*. Polonius — 'he's for a jig or a tale of bawdry or he sleeps' — would have preferred *Tempo* to high tragedy, no doubt. Or he might have slipped down the coast to dine in the Deer Park at Klampenborg and watch 'The Six English Jolly Girls', and similar delights of sylvan cabaret, as I used to do in happy summers before the war. Denmark will be my first Continental holiday of peace, if ever I have one. Meanwhile the lines of Humbert Wolfe, who knew the Danish castle like a lover, must be my consolation:

> I have seen great Kronborg standing in the red king's robes he
> wore
> when Hamlet, Prince of Denmark, was a prince at Helsingor —
> I have seen Fredensborg whiter than the pale white hand of a
> queen,
> and — a water-lily floating — Frederichsborg I have seen.

Humbert was a great scholar as well as wit and minstrel, but his history is here amiss, for Hamlet was never a Prince in this surviving Kronborg, which, though rose-red in certain sunset-lights, is by no means half as old as Time. Hamlet himself lived in the misty centuries of saga, probably five hundred years before the building of

Kronborg at Elsinore: this occurred about the time in which Shakespeare wrote his *Hamlet*. Humbert was also wrong in rhyming the Danish Helsingor with wore: it is Helsingör and you roll the 'o' and the 'r' to rhyme with 'were', almost as a Scotsman would say it. In any case we seem to have bettered the Danish, for Elsinore is a gentle and beautiful word.

The English singers of Elsinore have wrongly viewed it as craggy, presumably because marine castles are so often set on rocks. But here is no Tintagel or Rock of Dumbarton. The spit of land running up into the straits is flat enough and Shakespeare enormously romanticized the scene, which he certainly cannot have viewed with his own eyes. Horatio's talk of 'a high eastern hill' is nonsense: for the southern tip of Sweden is a featureless plain. Again

> the dreadful summit of the cliff
> That beetles o'er his base into the sea

is equally fictitious. Elsinore is by no means a Dover or a Beachy Head. But the myth of its precipitous nature lasted till Thomas Campbell in his 'Battle of the Baltic' bade us:

> Think of them that sleep,
> Full many a fathom deep
> By thy wild and stormy steep,
> Elsinore!

No, Elsinore is flat, and the Kronborg stands almost on sea level, mellow in its bricky towers as Hampton Court, draughty in its Great Court — which is by no means the world's best Open Air Theatre — and beautifully empurpled by lilac when the summer is young.

EMBRANGLEMENT

THE O.E.D. gives brangle as a form of wrangle. So embranglement should be, and sometimes is, a word for a fine tangle of argument and abuse. But, in the popular mind, the tangle can be material as well as mental. A correspondent tells me that it is a technical term of bell-ringers in certain areas. 'When a complicated piece of change-ringing is proceeding and one or another of the bells goes wrong, it is embranglement.' It is suggested that the jangle of the bells and the wrangle of the bellmen have both contributed to this usage. Country folk still use embranglement of any confusion or disaster. The same correspondent relates this of an incident in a Sussex wood. 'I was watching tree stumps being grubbed up with the aid of a traction engine. As sometimes happens on this sort of job the anchor holding the engine gave way and instead of the tree stump coming up, the engine lurched backward and rolled down a little bank, coming to rest at an angle of forty-five degrees or so with its fore-wheels cocked in the air. It looked rather a mess to me, but the engine-driver merely remarked that it was "a bloody fine embranglement".'

FALLOW

I N his poem on 'St. Philip and St. James' Christopher Smart, after announcing that

> Tansy, calaminth, and daisies
> On the river's margin thrive
> And accompany the mazes
> Of the stream that leaps alive,

further describes how

> Cowslips seize upon the fallow
> And the cardamine in white.

Cardamine is now more commonly known as Lady's Smock or Cuckoo Flower.

Fallow is an interesting word as well as agreeable to the ear. Originally it was the ploughed and harrowed land left unsown for a time and the colour of this fallow, pale or reddy brown, became another meaning of fallow itself. Fallow the adjective was applied to the paler species of British deer. The fallow-deer has a lighter hue than the red-deer, which has a deeper-tinted and truly rufous coat. Shakespeare used fallow of a greyhound. The Victorian poet F. W. Faber, writing of the Midlands, with dubious courtesy to Northants, where lurk some of the loveliest of England's stone-built villages, alluded to

> Fair Warwick's deep and shady brooks
> And blithe Northampton's meadow nooks —
> Tamest of counties!

He also mentioned the region's

> Scant shade and ruddy fallows.

Because fallow thus left unsown by man would soon show signs of nature-borne greenery, weed or grass, or of Smart's cowslips and cardamines, or because land cleaned by a crop of roots was known as 'green fallow', a confusion arose about fallow. Some writers certainly seem to think of it as land which, since unsown with crops, has been allowed to go to grass. Fallow for them is green, not grey or brown. What were Shakespeare's 'fallow leas'? Probably the once ploughed land that needs reploughing after being overrun by weeds.

The Duke of Burgundy in *Henry V* (V. 2), lamenting the sore plight of France, describes how,

> Her vine, the merry cheerer of the heart,
> Unpruned dies: her hedges even-pleach'd,
> Like prisoners wildly overgrown with hair,
> Put forth disorder'd twigs; her fallow leas
> The darnel, hemlock, and rank fumitory,
> Do root upon, while that the coulter rusts,
> That should deracinate such savagery.

The Scottish ballads bid the ploughman,

> Plough you hill and plough you dale,
> Plough you faugh and fallow.

But this is not an agricultural treatise. One thing certainly emerges, the good sense of retaining fallow as an adjective, since our countryside in winter is rich with such an extraordinary range of exquisite brown tints, for which our vocabulary is quite inadequate. The late Gavin Bone ('Cut is the branch that might have grown full straight, And burnéd is Apollo's laurel bough') who triumphantly showed that the Saxons could be poets and that Beowulf was not the only pebble on their Parnassus, wrote of their fallow-hafted knives.

FETTLE AND THRUNG

FETTLE survives mainly in the south of England as a noun, but rarely outside the phrase 'fine fettle.' This means condition. To fettle, more common in the north, is to make ready or to mend. A correspondent sends me the following: 'Cleg and fettle were verbs used in Northumberland meaning "to mend". I have never succeeded in finding any difference in meaning between the two words, but there is a difference. A Durham miner whom I questioned could do no better than "There's some things you clegs, and some you fettles". In Lancashire the engineering finishing-shops are called "fettling-shops", but "to fettle" seems never to mean "to finish" but rather "to repair".' He also sends me thrung, dialect past participle equivalent to thronged, meaning packed, cluttered up. Thus a cobbler's shop might be thrung with shoes waiting to be fettled.

FILEMOT AND MURREY

YOU can find the former with a Tudoresque variety of spellings. Filemot, philamot, philomot, phyllamort, feulamot show their orange-tawny hues down the centuries. For this is feuille morte, the sear, the yellow leaf, sometimes used as a noun, sometimes as an adjective for the ochred woods of autumn. It was in connection with ochre that I came across it recently in a poem by Mr. Andrew

Young. This singer was recently bemedalled for his good verses by the Royal Society of Literature and rightly so. Belonging to no clique and never pushing, he remains 'known to his own', in the old honorific phrase, but insufficiently quoted and seized by the anthologist. His particular genius is for the description of Britain's wintry scenes: he walks with a flashing vision among the vaporous hills and rain-swept fields, a natural laureate of the children of the mist. His Muse is as simple as Wordsworth's. He is a master of the monosyllable and as brief as lucid in his writing.

Of autumn he writes,

> The leaves hang on the boughs
> Filemot, ochreous
> Or fall, and strangely greet
> Green blades of winter wheat:
> The long buds of the beech
> Point where they cannot reach.

Browning talked in 'Sordello' of changing 'a murrey-coloured' robe for 'philamote' (surely the worst of the spellings). Murrey is mulberry-coloured and is not often used nowadays, except by those who are being deliberately 'period'. But Thomas Hardy wrote of 'murrey coloured brick'. That is odd, for brick is more often filemot. Medieval writing is deep-dyed in murrey. 'And where be my gownes of scarlet, sanguyn, murreye, and blewes sadde and lighte?' The usage of sad for dark bears a trifle hardly on Oxford, which surely had not yet to weep over lost causes when Hoccleve wrote this in 1412. Dickens has something to say about mulberry as the vulgarian's choice. 'If ever there was a wolf in a mulberry suit, that 'ere Job Trotter's him.' I cannot remember him using murrey. It is queer that the shorter word should pass, while the longer lives on. Usually it is brevity that survives.

English history is stained with murrey, London history in particular. Syon House, Chelsea, and the City had their mulberry trees as famous as Shakespeare's in New Place. The mulberry was a gift of the Renaissance, wandering hither from Persia by way of Italy. It was the raw material of silk and for textile purposes James I planted the famous Mulberry Garden, where now is Buckingham Palace. The two words, murrey and filemot, run well together and seem an echo from the most glorious of old walls and pleasaunces, sound drenched in sunshine. Autumn comes and the filemot tints replace the murrey, but, if you have read your way back into that Mulberry Garden where Sedley drank his Rhenish and sought company while Pepys managed to be 'mighty merry' among the arbours, you may have a mind empurpled by the history of rich and happy hours as surely as your fingers will be royally stained should you pick and eat the murrey in close or quadrangle.

FLEER

A FLEER was a smirk or grin, either mocking or deceitfully humble. Iago plays upon Othello's jealousy of Cassio thus:

> Do but encave yourself
> And mark the fleers, the gibes, and notable scorns,
> That dwell in every region of his face;
> For I will make him tell the tale anew
> Where, how, how oft, how long ago, and when
> He hath, and is again, to cope your wife.

Fleer in this instance is obviously a triumphant smirk. At other times and with other authors it is a Uriah Heep-ish grimace, a smile of bogus servility. Fawning and fleering go constantly together. Beaumont mocks the lot of the 'fallen sharer' (part-manager of a theatre) thus:

> Hath not his state almost as wretched been
> As his, that is ordained to write the grin
> After the fawn and fleer, shall be?

Johnson derides those who 'with their Court dog-tricks can fawn and fleer'. Shakespeare's fleering is derisive: his contemporaries mainly use the term for a pretended humility. It is an effective word and has oddly passed out of common usage. Browning, however, kept it in mind. This of Sordello:

> Amid his wild-wood sights he lived alone
> As if the poppy felt with him! Though he
> Partook the poppy's red effrontery
> Till Autumn spoiled their fleering quite with rain.

Here the fleer is of pride.

FLUMMOX

O U R English words for overthrown, and especially for confounded and confused, both of the dialect and of the dictionary kind, are rich and numerous. We are mithered and moidered, niddered and nithered, according to locality (mithered, I am told, is Nottinghamese, and may mean cold) and so forth and so on. Flummox is of general and long-standing usage. The dictionaries attribute it to English dialect, but Mr. Weller thought otherwise. 'If your governor don't prove a alleybi, he'll be what the Italians call reg'larly flummoxed.' 'Ingenious Italy' again! Whence Mr. Weller derived this derivation I cannot imagine. To say that Fascism was finally flummoxed seems inadequate: but the word is good for general perplexity and wit's end agitation.

FLUNKEY

A G R A N D word, as apt as toady for its theme. A possible derivation is to make it a corruption of 'flanker', i.e. of a man who stands at your side. (This is somewhat supported by John Wilson's mention of 'flunkey-flanked eckipages'.) The verb to flunk is a different matter, meaning to back down, renege, deny. 'He never flunked, he never lied', occurs in a much-quoted poem by John Hay, American diplomatist with a hand for rhyming. Flunkey entered the English language towards the end of the eighteenth century and became a favourite of Thomas Carlyle, who was much given to raging at flunkeyism and used flunkey both as adjective and noun.

> Thou and I, my friend, can, in the most flunkey world, make each of us one non-flunkey, one hero, if we like: that will be two heroes to begin with.

Of the execution of Charles I Carlyle wrote,

> This action of the English regicides did in effect strike a damp like death through the heart of Flunkeyism universally in this world, whereof Flunkeyism, Cant, Cloth-worship, or whatever ugly name it have, has gone about incurably sick ever since and is now, in these generations, at length very rapidly dying.

To which John Morley well replied that 'Cant is not slain in such easy terms by a single stroke of the republican headsman's axe'. But he wisely added, 'The very contrary of Carlyle's proposition as to death and damp might more fairly be upheld. For this at least is certain, that the execution of Charles I kindled and nursed for many generations a lasting flame of cant, flunkeyism, or whatever else be the right name of spurious and unmanly sentimentalism, more lively than is associated with any other business in our whole national history'.

That sums up for me the pro-Stuart sob-stuff still lingering in certain, mainly High Anglican and Catholic, circles. The fact of not applauding every aspect of Oliver's career and character does not induce me to public lamentation in Whitehall on January 30th, or to rejoicings upon Oakapple Day. Mention of the latter reminds me of an account in Mass Observation's volume on 'The Pub and the People' of strange celebrations of Oakapple Day at a Lancashire Inn, 'with a fine view of 39 factories'. A strange statue, more Mexican and Priapean than Caroline and Christian in style, was annually put up, framed with lime branches, honoured, and even kissed. Only natives kissed, but in old times you could buy the privilege with a gallon of beer for the aboriginals. Lines were then formally read out, including these, in equal celebration, it seems, of King Cotton and King Charles.

O yes, O yes, O yes, It is with pleasure I now behold,
A train of such truehearted Britons bold,
Commemorating in this grand Procession,
King Charles the Second's Happy Restoration.
The lively Genius of Tonge Fold in Trade
Which has for many ages been,
As all the world throughout proclaim,
The first origin of Counterpanes.
It was on this day his birth and restoration,
All was preserved from rumpish Usurpation.
Britannia's Sons, let us all due honours pay
In celebrating this auspicious day.
And you, young heroes, walk in procession grand,
All crowned with oak, each wearing a white wand.
Behave like men and commemorate
The happy restoration of King Charles the Great.
And sing God Save the King.

The image was then patted, called Charles, and kissed. On the whole a queer, convivial exhibition, and not so 'flunkey' as it seems. For it obviously derives from old pagan rites and must be a Counterpane-cum-counter-revolutionary adaptation of some primeval fertility junketings.

FRORE

THE Miltonic past participle of freeze hardly survives, though it was an occasional usage of most poets up till 1900. Indeed, the rather ugly and Latinate 'gelid' has had more life in our poetry. Frore has the right crisp sound for a nipping and eager air and brings to mind a day of black frost when the miry fields are turned to metal underfoot. Churchill made 'Frore January, leader of the year'. Swinburne used it well:

> Full-charged with old-world wonders,
> From dark Tintagel thunders
> A note that smites and sunders
>   The hard, frore fields of air.

Although the poem is about autumn, the last line has as much of essential winter in it as any Meredithian line about 'a wind with fangs'. The fliers were later to discover the whole and horrible truth about 'hard, frore fields of air'.

Sir John Squire in his poem on 'Rivers' proclaimed that the aged Brahmapootra, beyond the white Himalayas,

> Passes many a lamassery
> On rocks forlorn and frore.

Douglas Young, the Scottish Nationalist champion and excellent scholar of Hellenic, Gaelic, and other tongues, comments thus, among his many pleasing verses, upon Edinburgh's Calton Hill,

> A fine fantasy of the Whig literati
> To build a modern Athens in our frore islands.
> Those elegant oligarchs of the Regency period,
> Philhellenic nabobs and the Scots nobility.

But he further concludes, in good Nationalist style,

> Apeing foreign fashions is always derisible.

And he elsewhere asserts 'the brochs of Scotland seem to me examples of an architecture as remarkable as ancient Greek temple-building and no more absurd'. Brochs are dry-built circular forts or castles of stone.

Macbeth's place at Inverness was probably, in fact, one of Douglas Young's much admired brochs. Shakespeare, so kind to the local climate, omitted to call it frore, which it doubtless was at times.

FUSCOUS

PURE Latin, except for the intruding 'o', meaning dark and sombre. It is strange that so expressive a word should have been limited mainly to the technical lingo of Natural History. Weather and hill-scenery in rain often strike me as fuscous, but they are never called so. I was reminded of fuscosity by discovering it in a very queer passage written by Alfred Tennyson at the age of fourteen. The precocious boy found relief from the glooms and storms of his father's Rectory by writing a play in verse called *The Devil and the Lady*. The character Magus on finding the Devil disguised as a woman cries,

> How now, my Hellish Minister, dark child
> Of bottomless Hades: what rude waggery,
> What jejune, undigested joke is this,
> To quilt thy fuscous haunches with the flounced
> Frilled, finical delicacy of female dress?
> Hast thou dared to girdle thy brown sides
> And prop thy monstrous vertebrae with stays?
> Speak out, thou petticoated Solecism,
> Thou Hairy trifler.

There's vocabulary for you! The deeply and widely read boy had the trick of it early. Fuscous haunches powerfully suggest decaying venison to me. But who, if asked to name the author of,

> And prop thy monstrous vertebrae with stays

would have said Tennyson?

GALOSH

GALOSHES now are supposed to be droll when they are not being useful. That typical Little Man and comic curate of late Victorian farce The Private Secretary travelled with galoshes as well as with glass of milk and Bath bun for sustenance. Those seeking to mock Ibsen — a dreary form of fun — usually jest on the flag-staffs, top-hats, and galoshes, and the tooting of the steamers in the fiord. Leslie Henson once had a charming tale of guilty passion at work in a foreign triangle, De Hosband, De Vife, and De Oder. This last, in his amorous craft, used galoshes as 'sneakers' and became, for Henson, De Oder mit Goulash. But galoshes were once stout and manly articles. As galoches or galoshoes these were a kind of wooden clog or strong, protective boot. Then they became any kind of aid for the shelter of a light shoe. 'Coloshoos of velvet' appear in milady's shoe-cupboard in the seventeenth century. (The spelling of the word has had endless variations from galage and galache to colloshoes and golloshoes. Henson's goulash is the last fine careless recipe.) A gentleman's golloshoe, in the days before rubber, was an important item in his equipment. Sir Francis Throckmorton, a mid-seventeenth-century knight, had in his accounts a charge for galloshoes. So the Ibsenites and the Private Secretary were in brave company.

GECK, GIRN, AND GOWL

T H E fate of James Hogg's 'Bonnie Kilmeny' does not greatly stir me. Hogg, whether being fey or Jacobite, seems to me to have had less gumption than is to be expected in Ettrick Shepherds. However, he had the vocabulary of his time and place and it is a good one. The singer of Birniebouzle and Balmaquhapple was certain to have a lingo with the Border wind in it and the smell of neeps after rain. (Surely that exquisite aroma is essential Scotland: it has the sharp tang of so many Scottish things, of whisky, especially, and smoked fish, of pine-woods and peat.)

Hogg in the aforesaid 'Bonnie Kilmeny' has one passage containing the three words geck, girn, and gowl, which make a sombre and a striking trinity.

> He gowled at the carle and chased him away
>> To feed with the deer on the mountain gray.
> He gowled at the carle and he gecked at Heaven.

Previously the carle had 'girned amain'.

If a carle (or churl) girned amain at me, I should certainly deem it fair to geck and gowl, as well as girn, back at him. Taking them in order, geck, either as a verb for 'to mock' or as a noun for a person mocked, is by no means Scottish only. Cries Malvolio,

> Why have you suffered me to be imprisoned,
> Kept in a dark house, visited by the priest,
> And made the most notorious geck and gull
> That e'er invention played on?

The phrase 'geck and scorn' also appears in *Cymbeline*. Girn is supposed to be a mistaken form of grin. It means to show the teeth at, snarl, and generally grizzle and rail. Gowl is more vociferous and is a picturesque form of howl. One might put it this way: if you unfairly geck a fellow-creature, he first girns at you and then, if nothing happens, gowls.

GIFT

A CORRESPONDENT sent me the following note on Scottish habits.

'When the Dean Bridge was in course of building the two old villages (Dean and the Water of Leith Village) had the appearance of a busy human hive. The starting of work in the morning was regulated by the ancient practice of "beating the mett" — a custom as old as the village mills themselves. At the appointed hour one of the millers, approved and gifted in the matter of early rising, stood at the low Bridgend and beat the large corn measure, or mett, with the corn rolling-pin to a particular time or rhythm — a sound which was heard far up and down the valley. It was a sound signal as autocratic in its day as the modern time gun is now, and regulated every clock and watch in the neighbourhood.'

Mett was the word in my friend's mind. But what an exquisite phrase occurs also in the passage 'approved and gifted in the matter of early rising'. 'O wad some Pow'r the giftie gie us'! How many have this donation at birth and then live to be 'approved' in the use of the endowment? The world's great minds have had various opinions about the 'Gifting' of mankind, as the Scots would say. Meredith held the 'Sword of Common Sense' to be our surest gift and, on the whole, I agree with him. In the Book of Common Prayer continency is one gift, but charity is the most excellent. Question for the now modish 'quiz': Who first talked of 'the fatal gift of Beauty'? Answer: Byron in *Childe Harold* — 'Italia! oh Italia! thou who hast The fatal gift of beauty'.

Sleep, of course, has been the supreme gift in many a poet's lines. Elizabeth Barrett Browning spoke for all —

> Of all the thoughts of God that are
> Borne inward unto souls afar
>   Along the Psalmist's music deep,
> Now tell me if there any is,
> For gift or grace, surpassing this
>   'He giveth His beloved sleep'.

One could fill a volume with poignant outcry for the great gift of sleep. Far more pray for it, I fancy, than for the diligent Scot's austere ideal, namely, 'to be approved and gifted in the matter of early rising'.

GLOZE

G L O Z E was an Elizabethan favourite. It is akin to gloss, not the lustrous gloss, but the grammarians' explanation of a difficult word or passage. To explain may be, of course, not to explain; merely to gloss over or to gloze. Gloze thus comes to mean any kind of deceit or pretence. In an anonymous seventeenth-century poem on the familiar theme of rustic simplicity versus the subtlety and sin of courts, these latter are described as places

> Where strained sardonic smiles are glozing still
> And grief is forced to laugh against her will.

Shakespeare used gloze as comment or explain with a suggestion of quibble,

> No woman shall succeed in Salique land:
> Which Salique land the French unjustly gloze
> To be the realm of France!

John of Gaunt, observing that the tongues of dying men enforce attention like deep harmony, adds

> He that no more must say is listened more
> Than they whom youth and ease have taught to gloze.

Here glozing seems to be little worse than a mere glibness in light prattling. But Longaville's 'Now to plain dealing: lay these glozes by', suggests downright deceit.

GONGOOZLER

'AN idle and inquisitive person who stands staring for prolonged periods at anything out of the common. The word is believed to have its origin in the Lake District.'

This from the glossary of *Narrow Boat*, Mr. L. T. C. Rolt's much-appreciated book on our canals and their navigation.

W. H. Davies might have liked the word gongoozling for a practice he defended, but the habit became horrible when the 'out of the common' spectacle was air-raid damage.

GORDIAN

KEATS used Gordian with relish, even making it a verb for tie in knots. As an adjective he applied it in 'Lamia' to bodies as well as strings. There was that serpent which Hermes, 'bent warm on amorous theft', found instead of a more normal and covetable companion in the woods of Crete. Keats certainly made 'a very good report of the worm', as Cleopatra's clown said of another asp. It was

> a palpitating snake,
> Bright and cirque-couchant in a dusky brake;
> She was a gordian shape of dazzling hue,
> Vermilion-spotted, gold and green and blue,
> Striped like a zebra, freckled like a pard,
> Eye'd like a peacock and all crimson-barr'd,
> And full of silver moons. . . .

Our eyes dazzle indeed. Plainly, here was rather more than 'a pretty worm'. Amateurs of the glamorous contortionism, which used to be seen in the elegant and Cochranesque revues, will rejoice in this passage, though it be scarcely Keats at his best. What a tangle of words! I fancy that in all the history of showmanship no star of contortion or Boneless Wonder has ever been billed as both gordian and cirque-couchant.

Gordius was a Phrygian king whose pastime was knotting, one specimen of which he left as his masterpiece. Alexander the Great, sensibly refusing to break his thumb-nails on this piece of intricate nuisance, sliced it with his sword. As the Oracle had prophesied the conquest of Asia to the man who loosened the knot, it is a surprising reflection on the initiative of the time that nobody had taken this short cut before. Gordius and Alexander between them contributed a word which has remained and might be more employed. As an adjective for 'properly tied up', as well as for intricately twisted, it sounds and looks imposingly.

HABERDASHER

THE origin of this handsome Elizabethan fellow is obscure. He was at first a hatter and only later on became the general draper, the dealer in laces and ribbons and petty clothing of all kind. Autolycus, a strolling-haberdasher to us, was not such to Shakespeare, who mentions the word but once, when he alludes (*Henry VIII*, V. 3) to a haberdasher's wife in a crowd with a 'Pinkt porringer on her head'. The Tudor gallant would pay high for his lady's haberdashery, forty shillings or more, an enormous sum in those days. But for that he expected an exclusive model, 'the impression extant but that morning', as Dekker puts it in an amusing passage in *The Gull's Horne-Booke*. He is explaining the art of behaving badly in a theatre and has pointed out that the most offensive thing to do is to leave your seat (at the side of the stage) as noisily as possible during the play and 'draw what troop you can from the stage after you'. If you do not move then 'my counsel is that you turn plain ape. Take up a rush, and tickle the earnest ears of your fellow gallants, to make other fools fall a-laughing; mew at passionate speeches; blare at merry; find fault with the music; whew at the children's action; whistle at the songs; and, above all, curse the sharers, that whereas the same day you had bestowed forty shillings on an embroidered felt and feather, Scotch fashion, for your mistress in the court, or your punk in the city, within two hours after you encounter with the very same block on the stage, when the haberdasher swore to you the impression was extant but that morning'. (The sharers would be called 'the management'.)

The hatter, no longer monopolizing the great name of haberdasher, still uses block, felt, and feather and even, for sporting modes, 'Scotch fashion' as well as French. But it is rarely now that the gentry mew, blare, and whew at a play. Not long ago this was 'Scotch fashion' in the Glasgow music-halls and perhaps still is. I remember one Saturday night in that city when the mewing and whewing were so fierce that no turn ever ended as arranged.

Returning to our haberdasher, we at length find him turning up as that symbol of strict and Puritanical propriety in Samuel Butler's famous Book of Montreal.

> The Discobolus hath no gospel,
> But my brother-in-law is haberdasher to Mr. Spurgeon.
> Oh God, Oh Montreal.

The Tudor haberdasher was no Puritan. He served both the macaronis and the punks with delicate, curious and costly head-pieces and was very much the tradesman-about-town.

HALCYON

I RETURN to this word, discussed in my first volume, with apologies for an error. I had thought that 'halcyon beaks' meant long, sharp noses. A correspondent, Miss Sylvia Carr, has sent me an interesting correction.

In Shakespeare's day and much earlier Halcyons or Kingfishers were stuffed, with their wings outstretched and hung from the eaves of houses to act as wind vanes. This use of Kingfishers was widespread in both England, North France, and Brittany, and widespread also was the belief that Kingfishers could foretell the weather. I do not know if this superstition originated from the Greek fable, or not. It is mentioned in several books and plays in the fifteenth and sixteenth centuries. Marlowe has a delightful reference to it in *The Jew of Malta* when one of his characters says:

How stands the wind? Into what corner peers my Halcyon's bill?

I feel that in *King Lear* Kent had the Halcyon's uncanny fore-knowledge in mind when he spoke of courtiers, noting their ability to twist and spin with every puff of wind.

> Such smiling rogues . . .
> Renege, affirm, and turn their Halcyon beaks
> With every gale and vary of their masters.

After all an experienced courtier should know not only which way the wind is blowing but which way it is likely to blow next!

The most modern reference to Kingfishers as weather vanes, which I have been able to find, is in one of Burke's speeches; he says 'This sanguine little Kingfisher (not prescient of the storm as by his instinct he ought to be)'.

Halcyon is a word confusing as well as enchanting. When were the 'halcyon days'? The old idea was a magic calm in mid-winter or early spring, but Shakespeare's 'Expect St. Martin's summer, halcyon days' put them in the autumn, gossamer-time. (See note on 'Attercop'.)

HAPPY

ONE form of Servicemen's irony is to take a word and then give it an exactly opposite meaning. For example, happy was used in the war to signify complete misery, shell-happy replacing the old shell-shocked. Here is a passage from a Canadian soldier's letter to his wife written after the terrific struggle round Caen.

> Can't say much about what goes on here now. When things get straightened out I'll tell you all about it. The Germans here

are not the surrendering type. For some reason they are prepared to get killed — and that's what *will* happen. They must be pretty shell-and-bomb happy by now. A bomb- or shell-happy case is so bad that to see one almost makes you feel as bad. The victim of it can't talk, just shakes and trembles. The eyes seem to pop out, too, and the case can hardly walk unassisted. All the nerves in the body go haywire. But after a little rest they are okay again.

Just when I had read this a soldier back from Burma started to talk to me about men who become 'jungle-happy', by which he meant overwhelmed by heat, loneliness, and pests of all kinds. Sand-happy was similarly used of men who have been affected by the deserts of the Middle East. There is a certain parallel here with the use of 'punch-drunk' to mean half-stunned by a blow. The dictionaries give 'slightly drunk' as one meaning of happy.

HAZING

R E C O R D S of American and Canadian Student Life usually have some reference to the violent form of ragging called by them hazing. Of General Marshall it was recently written, 'At West Point he had survived a bayoneting by an over-enthusiastic upper-classman in his first year without revealing the loutish hazer's name'. Haze is another of the English words early transported and long retained by Americans. For an English writer in 1630 it was natural to comment on 'that custome to beat and to box and with strange words and out-cryes to hazen children'. Now the hazer has gone entirely West.

MOST of our dances are aliens. A fine romantic rout they are, bergamask and lavolta, rigadoon and saraband, to mention but a few. But our native frisks can look imposing too. What of heydeguise, or heydeguy, spelt alternatively with hay for hey, reminding us of Marlowe's antic hay?

> By wells and rills in meadows green
> We nightly dance our heydeguise
> And to our fairy king and queen
> We chant our moonlight harmonies.

This comes from an anonymous seventeenth-century dithyramb on 'Robin Goodfellow', which also contains the nice verb 'to whirry', a compound of whirl and hurry.

> More swift than wind away I go
> O'er hedge and lands,
> Through pools and ponds
> I whirry, laughing 'Ho, ho, ho'.

Heydeguisers probably whirried a good deal in the practice of their ho-de-ho sport. Drayton, too, knew the antic.

> While some the ring of bells and some the bagpipe ply,
> Dance many a merry round and many a heydeguy.

Folk dances are plainly one of the most strenuous forms of exercise and those who have endured 'a running set' are athletes indeed. Drayton's allusion to 'many a heydeguy' suggests that a singleton of this kind might have been easy going, but Puck or Robin Goodfellow on the 'whirry' would not have been satisfied with anything merely gentle or static.

HO-GO

THIS is seventeenth-century English for Haut-Goût, a piquant flavour. 'No Hogoes to make the sauce pleasant and the stomach sharp.' Fuller called garlic a 'delicious Hault-gust'. The thoroughly Anglicized form has the good hearty smack of bread and cheese and pickled onions, a ho-go for the hobo. As a pickle-fancying, relish-relishing, Worcester-Sauceful nation we should have kept Ho-go.

HUNGER-BITTEN

IT was the opinion of Job's Comforter, Bildad the Shuhite, that the wicked man does not prosper. Subject to guns, snares, and nets he is also menaced by many another doom. 'His strength shall be hunger-bitten and destruction shall be ready at his side.' Hungry is, by itself, a powerful and biting adjective, but hunger-bitten is tremendous. It has the fangs of the east wind in it and calls up the 'looped and window'd raggedness' of the vagrant poor as well as the pinched and pallid frame of the Scots' 'poortith', English poverty. I suppose hunger-bitten was popular English at the time of the Authorized Version: this kind of double-barrelled, yet simple, epithet lingers yet upon the land. Henry Williamson, writing of the menace from floods to the winter-wheat on his Norfolk farm, mentioned in one of his articles that, if the worst occurred, the locals would call his crop 'water-slain'. Water-slain is to drowned as hunger-bitten to hungry: it crowns distress and disaster.

By a curious coincidence I had only just written this when, looking at the poems of Dunbar, I found slain applied to the effect of 'too much water' on the vegetable world. Of the changefulness of things Dunbar wrote that the day which comes in fresh as a peacock's feather turns to sting one like an adder. He continued,

> Yesterday fair up sprang the flouris
> This day thai ar all slane with schouris;
> And fowlis in forrest that sang cleir
> Now walkis with a drery cheir.
> Full cauld ar baith thair beddis and bouris.

The blossoms water-slain, the birds hunger-bitten. Since writing this note I have just discovered the modern scientist's translation of hunger-bitten into his odious jargon. It is 'suffering from avitaminosis', which is certainly a bellyful of syllables.

HURRICANO

T H I S Spanish word, specially applied to the storms of the West Indies, seems more effective in its early, un-Anglicized, four-syllable form. It was also furicano, which is even better. Shakespeare knew it only as hurricano. Cries Troilus,

> Not the dreadful spout
> Which shipmen do the hurricano call,
> Constring'd in mass by the almighty sun,
> Shall dizzy with more clamour Neptune's ear
> In his descent than shall my prompted sword
> Falling on Diomed.

The thing was a column of water to Shakespeare, not just a wind or tempest. Hurricano is again linked with spout in the Storm Scene in *King Lear*,

> Blow, winds, and crack your cheeks! rage! blow!
> You cataracts and hurricanoes, spout
> Till you have drench'd our steeples, drown'd the cocks!
> You sulphurous and thought-executing fires,
> Vaunt-couriers to oak-cleaving thunderbolts,
> Singe my white head! And thou, all-shaking thunder,
> Strike flat the thick rotundity o' the world!

Here is polysyllabic poetry at its most vehement. Just after hearing this cataract of speech in a revival of *King Lear* I happened to re-read Synge's superb one-act play *The Shadow of the Glen*, with its great talk of a hurricano's wet and windy leavings on the Wicklow hills. Says Norah Burke to Michael Dara,

> for what good is a bit of a farm with cows on it, and sheep on the back hills, when you do be sitting looking out from a door the like of that door, and seeing nothing but the mists rolling down the bog, and the mists again and they rolling up the bog, and hearing nothing but the wind crying out in the bits of broken trees were left from the great storm, and the streams roaring with the rain.

Surely that drives into the very heart of a streaming sou'-wester. What is interesting is to compare the two methods of storm-painting, the polysyllabic and highly-coloured with the brief and the bare. In four lines, Shakespeare has one word of five syllables, two of four, and four of three. In Synge's passage there are seventy words of one syllable and a dozen of two, mostly participles of simple monosyllabic verbs such as sit, see, and hear. Yet Synge, no less, could stage a cataract and set a hurricano whistling upwards to the gallery.

IMBROUN

THIS word may look strange, but it is only Miltonic for embrown. 'In the Garden of Eden'

> the crisped Brooks,
> Rowling on Orient Pearl and sands of Gold,
> With mazie error under pendant shades
> Ran Nectar, visiting each plant, and fed
> Flours worthy of Paradise, which not nice Art
> In Beds and curious Knots, but Nature boon
> Powrd forth profuse on Hill and Dale and Plaine,

Both where the morning Sun first warmly smote
The open field, and where the unpierc't shade
Imbround the noontide Bowrs: Thus was this place,
A happy rural seat of various view.

Pope has the same verb in a passage which surprisingly and charmingly forecasts the breaking-up of parkland at the Nobleman's Seat for the needs of modern war.

Another age shall see the golden Ear
Embrown the Slope, and nod on the Parterre,
Deep Harvests bury all his pride has plann'd,
And laughing Ceres re-assume the land.

The second couplet shows Pope out of his urban element, as an Augustan poet, but none the less at the supreme of his felicity.

Imbroun, Embroun, why mention so plain a word? It is worth realizing, surely, how much value can be added to a simple noun or adjective by making it a verb with a prefix. Shakespeare was continually at it, incorpsing a rider with his horse or distasting farewell kisses with the salt of broken tears. Or, rising higher, one meets and revives such stately beauties as incarnadine, imparadise, unparagon.

Brown is an adjective of humble service and, though not mean, makes no particular appeal to the ear. (Londoners making it Brahn, Bre-own, and almost Bryan, play hell with it, as I am frequently made aware.) To put im- or em- in front of it does considerably add to its stature and dignity and creates a verb worthy of harvest and of autumn. That is sufficient compliment.

IMPERIAL

THE soaring second syllable of this adjective and the following roll of the liquids, 'r' and 'l', give it a properly commanding power. It is worth while noticing that, while Empire seems an ugly and even a weak word, fit only for the prose of the less gifted publicists, imperial swims finely on the flood of the loftiest verse. The 'i' in

Empire is unpleasing and the 'r' disappears, at least when Englishmen are speaking. So from our political platforms we are accustomed to hear of Empiyah or even of Empah, which are both an affliction. But it is natural and easy to enjoy the strong music of imperial, a word whose quality of sound seems to lift it far above the material trappings of terrestrial dominion. Even the Grand Babylons of the hotel-industry have not killed the glory of Wordsworth's line about the origin of the human child with heaven all about him,

> And that imperial palace whence he came.

The epithet survives the hard usages of caterer and showman, sur- vives indeed with credit wherever it appears. Shakespeare's 'Im- perial votaress' is perfect for royal dedication and 'the swelling act of the imperial theme' has mystery as well as majesty about it. A Caesar is dignified by being called imperial, obvious though the adjective may be in his case. Shakespeare could not wring much poetry out of empire and turned at times to empery which now seems to be a piece of 'poetese'. Empyreal, of course, is celestial and has nothing to do with Empire, but, with similarity of sound, it can have the imperial ring, as Wordsworth knew:

> All strength — all terror, single or in bands,
> That ever was put forth in personal form —
> Jehovah — with his thunder, and the choir
> Of shouting Angels, and the empyreal thrones —
> I pass them unalarmed. Not Chaos, not
> The darkest pit of lowest Erebus,
> Nor aught of blinder vacancy, scooped out
> By help of dreams, can breed such fear and awe
> As fall upon us often when we look
> Into our Minds, into the Mind of Man,
> My haunt, and the main region of my song.

These, despite the weakness of 'often' in the last line but two, are tremendous lines and modern enough in their presage of psycho- analysis to be worth quoting when our intellectual comedians are having their rather paltry fun at the expense of Old Daddy Words- worth.

Poor Imperial sank badly when it came to be applied to a miniature beard, which nowadays conveys an air of affectation. An agreeable synonym for this kind of Imperial was recently supplied by a Dublin barber who, confronted by an aesthetic young man equipped with one of these chin-trifles, exclaimed,

> Ah, come right in, now. We've a fine way here surely with those fancy bushes.

Imperial should have been excluded from the coiffeurs' world. Its proper life is among crowns and lilies and palaces and in the more exalted reaches of blank verse.

INTELLIGENCE

A WEARISOME number of obvious jokes must have been made about the Service men who have to admit an appointment to 'Intelligence'. The Services so often employ bad new English that it is interesting to find them in this matter of Intelligence to be good conservatives, even antiquarians. To the Elizabethans intelligence was news and not 'nous'. I do not think that Shakespeare ever employed the word in the sense most common to-day, that of wisdom or perspicuity. He did, indeed, use it especially of military information and of martial communications. 'Advise the Duke,' says Cornwall at the end of *King Lear*, when the war is on, 'Advise the Duke where you are going, to a most festinate preparation; we are bound to the like. Our posts shall be swift and intelligent between us.' Perhaps the use of intelligence which strikes us as most surprisingly up-to-date occurs in one of the Chorus Speeches in *Henry V* (This piece will now, I suppose, be labelled by shrewd showmen as 'The Play of the Film': I have never forgotten seeing a copy of *Tess of the D'Urbervilles* on the bookstall at Victoria Station commended to the reader as 'The Book of the Play', the play being a version then on view at a surburban theatre!) But to return to the other kind of intelligence (or lack of it), here is the passage. Concerning the 'D' Day prior to Agincourt, Chorus announces:

For now sits Expectation in the air,
And hides a sword from hilts unto the point
With crowns imperial, crowns, and coronets,
Promis'd to Harry and his followers.
The French, advised by good intelligence
Of this most dreadful preparation,
Shake in their fear: and with pale policy
Seek to divert the English purposes.

'Good intelligence' is much of our moment. It is the R.A.F.'s 'pukka gen'. 'Gen' has been attributed to genuine, but, as Eric Partridge points out, pukka gen in that case becomes a pleonasm, being really 'genuine genuine'. He attributes 'gen' to the phrase 'for the general information of all ranks'. But might not 'gen' be simply short for intelligence? It would then be no innovation at all, but as old as the Tudors and their posts and spies.

Shakespeare also used the word in the famous Sonnet on the rival poet,

He, nor that affable familiar ghost
Which nightly gulls him with intelligence.

Here the 'gen' is not so pukka, but it is the old 'newsy' intelligence, which is far removed from the modern intelligence of the intelligentzia.

INVEIGLE

W H A T a number of words one uses without troubling to think about them! Inveigle, for example. An attractive, expressive word for to snare and to lead on with lures. Originally it meant to blind; the 'veigle' element is found in the French 'aveugle'. And why aveugle? Because of the late Latin *ab oculis*, 'without eyes'. So the journey from the oculist's consulting-room to a fair lady's blinding inveiglements is, in its queer way, direct.

ASMINE

THIS — the Arab's Yasmin which made music for Flecker — is a happy gift from the East, whether we call it jasmin or jessamine. Poets weave it constantly into their floral patterns. It is the delicate flower, exquisitely wan. The common poetical epithet for it is faint. Shelley had it so, to Milton it was pale, to Wordsworth pure; to Hood, taking a lustier view, it was sweet and owning many loves. Matthew Arnold conceived it as an essential part of summer's pride

> Too quick despairer, wherefore wilt thou go?
> Soon will the high Midsummer pomps come on,
> Soon will the musk carnations break and swell,
> Soon shall we have gold-dusted snapdragon,
> Sweet-William, with his homely cottage-smell
> And stocks in fragrant blow;
> Roses that down the alleys shine afar,
> And open, jasmine-muffled lattices,
> And groups under the dreaming garden-trees
> And the full moon, and the white evening star.

It is particularly the window-climbing flower. Tennyson set it swaying to the melody of *Maud*.

> All night has the casement jessamine stirred
> To the dancers dancing in tune;
> Till a silence fell with the waking bird,
> And a hush with the setting moon.

Jessamine trips in so featly as a dactyl into any catalogue of blossoms that it was rarely forgotten in the days when poets were not ashamed of making an agreeable noise.

JO

WHEN asked what the Jo meant in 'John Anderson, my jo', I could only reply rather vaguely, 'Friend'. This indeed it frequently did mean, but the word began as an abbreviation of Joy. So it was properly used in 'The Gude and Godlie Ballatis',

> In dulci jubilo, now let us sing with mirth and jo.

Later the Jo that was also a Joy became mainly personal in Scottish application, but the usage does not seem to have travelled far south. Allan Ramsay sang of his 'Jo Janet'. Scottish song continues to use jo in the sense of dear companion or lover. Violet Jacob, singer of Angus and the Mearns, spells it Joe.

> My grannie spent a merry youth,
> She never wanted for a Joe.

The word appears also in the rhymes of baby-talk and there, I think, most happily. Jo for a laughing child seems apter than for an adult and frosty-powed Anderson.

LAP

LAP for wrap (no relation to the lapping of milk or lapping of waves on the beach), has been brought to my notice as proper Lancashire English by so good an authority on the subject as Mr. T. Thompson. In his profession of book-binding he had to work upon some old parish-registers and found there frequent references to 'lapping in wool' at funerals. To help the wool-trade, he says, there was once a law that corpses should be lapped in wool. Wool, not cotton? Alas, poor Lancashire! Was Yorkshire 'putting something over' with this wool-sack legislation? Thompson added that in Bury they still often say 'lap it up' instead of 'wrap it up'. Lancashire has retained another old English word for lapping houses and even babies. That is to hele or hill for to cover. An old woman would say 'hill that chilt up' in cold weather. We find the same usage in the name Hillier or Hiller, which is an occupational name. A 'hiller' hilled people by covering their roofs.

The old lap is Miltonic. The author of 'L'Allegro' asked to be lapped in soft Lydian airs. It was Hazlitt who invented 'lapped in luxury', but that may have come from the physical lap. The Scots have hap instead of, or in addition to, lap. When describing his happiness in coming from peasant stock Lewis Grassic Gibbon wrote that he was:

> Conscious of an overweening pride that mine (origin) was so and so and that the land was so closely and intimately mine — my mother used to hap me in a plaid in harvest-time and leave me in the lea of a stook while she harvested . . . .

LAPIDATE

EVERY householder knows what dilapidations cost, even though the word be not fully earned by the actual parting of stone from stone. The hurling of stone on stone or after stone (in the direction of a target) is, on the other hand, lapidation, a word less known and employed. I was amused to find Bernard Shaw using this term in an account of an assault with large stones made upon himself by some Scottish bairns who presumably knew not whom they stoned, and how potent the missile. 'Their notion of play', he wrote in *Everybody's Political What's What*, 'was to throw stones at a strange elderly gentleman with a beard, defying him meanwhile with war-cries describing him opprobriously as a Beaver.' He added, 'If the Scottish laddies who lapidated me had been organized as Boy Scouts, they would never have dreamed of treating me as St. Stephen was treated 2000 years ago'. (G.B.S. is strongly pro-Scout.) Lapidate has the good authority of Scott and Meredith and would give dignity to the stoning of old tin-kettles and other familiar games of the pebbly shore.

LEERY

LEERY for evasive, cunning, or wideawake is still good rustic English. To the fowler the wood-pigeon remains a leery bird. Presumably leery, like the verb and noun leer, is derived from the old, forgotten use of leer or lear, leery or leary which meant face or cheek. A correspondent has reminded me of Malory's 'lytel bratchet' which leaped upon Sir Tristram and 'licked his learys'. A leer is supposed to have been a glance over your cheek, an oblique or askance look, a lewd or mischievous grimace. On the whole, leer or lear seems to have gone downhill: at first it was a cautious glance and later on it became a sinister and coarse one. Leery, in its first sense, was an early casualty. When Falstaff says that Mrs. Ford gives 'the leer of invitation', is he referring to the sly look or the kissable cheek? It is noteworthy that while leery, once cheek, became a look, cheek in our time has proceeded to be a whole mood of impudence and pert audacity. Leer or lear was also an adjective for empty or hungry and may linger still as such in country places.

LIBERAL

LIBERAL has always seemed to me an adjective most fascinating in the variety of its uses. I was at one time much allured by the announcement of 'Liberal Table' in the old advertisements of boarding-houses. Two eggs for breakfast? Has this nice boast of plenty entirely vanished among war-time limitations on food in the larder and on space in the newspapers? The use of liberal in Shakespeare alone would suffice for pages of comment and quotation. With him it could be applied equally to the rough peasant and the refined scholar. Prospero followed 'the liberal arts', i.e. those with no taint of technical or financial utility, the pursuits of a wealthy, leisured gentleman. (Dr. Johnson defined liberal as 'becoming a gentleman', the word being not yet applied to the Whigs whom he deemed no gentlemen at all.) Yet Shakespeare could equally speak of 'liberal shepherds', meaning peasants gross of speech. It is noteworthy that the master-dramatist could stop in the middle of a most poignant passage, Queen Gertrude's description of Ophelia's watery end, to drag in a bawdy jest upon the name given by those English 'liberals' in their taverns and steadings to a certain kind of flower, the long purple. Anything less dramatically apposite than this introduction at such a moment (and in Denmark!) of a smutty joke beloved of English hinds and drovers could hardly be imagined. Yet what a lovely speech remains!

Liberal, therefore, means free of mind, free of speech, and free of purse. A man could be 'profane and liberal' just as much as he could be liberal and charitable.

> Kent, in the Commentaries Caesar writ,
> Is term'd the civil'st place of all this isle:
> Sweet is the country, beauteous, full of riches,
> The people liberal, valiant, active, wealthy.

This, probably not Shakespearean, was a piece of special pleading made to Jack Cade, playing on Kentish pride. Liberal, to the translators of the Bible, meant generous and was contrasted in Isaiah with churlish. The churl devises wicked devices to destroy the poor, but 'the liberal deviseth liberal things and by liberal things shall he stand'. This shows the width of meaning possessed by liberal in Elizabethan and Jacobean times, for it also meant licentious and was commonly applied to seducers.

Liberal, as a political term, came to us early in the nineteenth century. In 1859 John Bright said 'I am for Peace, Retrenchment, and Reform, the watchword of the great Liberal Party thirty years ago'. The term was beginning to supplant the name of Whig in the eighteen-twenties, having arrived from Europe.

W h a t an extraordinary origin has Lungis, the lanky lout, if the O.E.D. is correct — and who impugns it? — in its attribution to Longinus, the apocryphal name of the tall centurion who pierced the side of Jesus with a spear. Lungis became the long and clumsy man, the lubberly creature. Cries the Citizen's Wife over Ralph the Apprentice in *The Knight of the Burning Pestle* after one of his romantically intended struggles,

> Oh, husband, here's Ralph again! — Stay, Ralph, again, let me speak with thee. How dost thou, Ralph? art thou not shrewdly hurt? the foul great lungies laid unmercifully on thee: there's some sugar-candy for thee. Proceed; thou shalt have another bout with him.

It might occur, but does not, in the famous Rabelaisian list of oafs, knaves, and blockheads, which includes, among others,

> Prating gablers, lickorous gluttons, freckled bittors, mangie rascals, slie knaves, drowsie loiterers, slapsauce fellowes, slabberdegullion druggels, lubbardly lowts, cozening foxes, paultrie customers, sycophant varlets, drawlatch hoydons, flouting milksops, staring clowns, forlorn snakes, ninnie lobcocks, scurvie sneaksbies, fondling fops, base lowns, sawcie coxcombs, idle lusks, scoffing braggards, noddie meacocks, blockish grutnols, doddipol joltheads, jobbernol goosecaps, foolish loggerheads, slutch calflollies, grouthead gnatsnappers, lobdotterels, gaping changelings, codshead loobies, woodcock slangams, ninnyhammer flycatchers, and noddiepeak simpletons.

This is a glorious list, with which compare some modern Scottish specimens under the heading of 'Perjink and Others'. While missing lungis, it does include lusks, who are sloths. To lusk is to be idle, to be a lusk or luskish; the term has the right sound of a yawn, and is almost a collision of lie and bask. Another good old word for a loafing lout is gangrel. Lungis was linked with lusks and gangrels in Blunt's *Glossographia*, 1687. The Scottish gangrel is a tramp or wanderer: Violet Jacob sings of the gangrel loon who knows the Sidlaw Hills by heart as well as by eye. The English gangrel is a long loose-limbed, shuffling creature. In short, another lungis.

MALACHITE

A STONE resembling the leaf of the mallow in colour and so an adjective for that kind of green. I mention it because a previous note of mine on 'greenth' lamented the limitations of the English writer who wishes to describe green things without recourse to the Latinities, verdant and virid. To this a correspondent has replied,

> First I would place Emerald (almost as liquid as that gem-word Vermilion, and with more depth) — then Beryl, Myrtle, Sea-green and Olive, and that one which gives the hardness of stone after its liquid start, *malachite*. (That wonderful colour ecstasy in A.E.'s poem 'Michael' where Michael hangs over the cliff edge and sees the swirling foam: 'Whirlpools of opal, lace of light, Strewn o'er the quivering Malachite', brings me a few lines later to one of the most beautiful of the green tints — jade.)

These are fit to be matched against a list of blues,

> Azure, Hyacinth, Sapphire and Sky, Speedwell, Forget-me-not, Powder and Peacock, and Watchet.

Much of this is excellent, but I doubt whether the argument is quite fair. Of course if you are going to make an epithet of every noun describing a blue or green thing, the resources of the language are immense, but are Beryl, Myrtle, Speedwell, and Forget-me-not really in use as adjectives? If I wrote of a lady with forget-me-not eyes beside a beryl sea under a speedwell sky fringed with myrtle pastures, would it be fully understood that I was not trying to be funny?

87

MAMMET

I HAD always thought that Shakespeare's mammet was in some way derived from mamma and maternity. 'A whining mammet' (Capulet's angry name for Juliet) would be in that case a child, while Hotspur's 'play with mammets' suggests dolls, which children mother. But mammet appears to be a corruption of maumet and maumet is Mahomet. Since Mahomedans were once regarded as typically idolatrous, a maumet was an idol and later applied to dolls contemptuously and next to naughty or foolish children. Mammet and maumetry merit a second youth in order to diversify the threadbare and monotonous jargon of our politics. Let Labour indict the Tory mammets of class and privilege or the Liberal mammetry of obsolete Cobdenism; let Toryism hit back at the dreary mammet of nationalization. Surely the poor, forswunk word Shibboleth might be given a rest and mammet, though not identical, restored to employment.

MANDRAGORA AND MITHRIDATES

SHAKESPEARE'S mandragora is a drowsy syrup in its own right. The very syllables are a lullaby. It is the same article as the mandrake; the longer form of this plant represents its soothing qualities, while the shorter is usually associated with the shrieks it was alleged to give out when plucked. In Elizabethan poetry the mandrake is forever raising its eerie voice; its screams and ululations go with moonlight and witchcraft and all things dark and sinister. To ward off the fatal effects of sinister foods and potions one could take a mithridate. This, of course, derived from the ancient King Mithridates of Pontus who, like our own James I, went in great and constant dread of assassins. But, whereas James wore padded clothes as his defence against a stiletto, Mithridates took a poison-course and so pickled his inside that it was at length deemed proof against all such banes. Hence mithridate for any kind of antidote.

I came across the usage in an exquisite piece of pastoral-sentimental among the Essays and Characters of John Stephens (1615). Included in his Arcadian picture of the Shepherd is this passage:

> He comprehends the true pattern of a moderate wise man; for as a shepherd, so a moderate man hath the supremacy over his thoughts and passions; neither hath he any affection of so wild a nature, but he can bring it into good order, with an easy whistle. The worst temptation of his idleness teaches him no further mischief, than to love entirely some nut-brown milk-maid, or hunt the squirrel or make his cosset wanton. He may turn many rare esteemed physicians into shame and blushing; for whereas they, with infinite compounds and fair promises, do carry men to death the furthest way about; he with a few simples preserves himself and family to the most lengthened sufferance of nature. Tar and honey be his mithridates and syrups; the which, together with a Christmas carol, defend his desolate life from cares and melancholy.

A cosset was a pet lamb and gave us our verb for fondle, pet, or spoil. (See note on Cosset.) Wanton here is a verb meaning to gambol or frisk.

The English countryside in English letters has strange contrasts. Either it is moon-blanched, hag-ridden, and resounding with the eldritch shrieks of plucked mandragora or else it is the basking-ground of idyllic shepherds with their simple minds immune from the corruptions of the Court and with honey and tar their simple mithridates against a physical infection.

MANTLE

THE Tudor men used mantle as a verb in fascinating ways. It occurs, strangely, in a particularly beautiful sonnet of Spenser's on the conflict of sacred and profane love:

> Oft when my spirit doth speed her bolder wings,
> In mind to mount up to the purest sky,
> It down is weighed with thought of earthly things
> And clogg'd with burden of mortality,
> Where, when that sovran Beauty it doth spy,
> Resembling heaven's glory in her light,
> Drawn with sweet Pleasure's bait, it back doth fly,
> And unto heaven forgets his former flight.
> There my frail Fancy, fed with full delight,
> Doth bathe in bliss and mantleth most at ease,
> Ne thinks of other heaven, but how it might
> Her heart's desire with more contentment please.

I said it occurred 'strangely' because here the common meaning of to mantle will not apply. Apparently mantle was one of the numerous terms taken from hawking by the poets of the time. The perched hawk mantled when he stretched his wings out over his outstretched legs for gentle exercise. So the mantling of Spenser's fancy was a kind of lounging in delight. The other and commoner significance of the verb mantle is derived from the secondary meaning of mantle the noun: this was used for the human cloak and also for the cloak of foam or scum on water. Poor Tom in *King Lear* 'drinks the green mantle of the standing pool'. Ariel speaks of the 'filthy-mantled' pool beyond Prospero's cell. So it is natural for Prospero soon after to speak of the ignorant fumes that mantle the reason of erring men. Most striking usage, perhaps, and probably most familiar occurs in Gratiano's speech at the beginning of *The Merchant of Venice*:

There are a sort of men, whose visages
Do cream and mantle like a standing pond
And do a wilful stillness entertain,
With purpose to be dressed in an opinion
Of wisdom, gravity, profound conceit;
As who should say, 'I am Sir Oracle,
And, when I ope my lips, let no dog bark!'

So mantle was further employed for blushing and Spenser's lady might have mantled with emotion while his Fancy mantled, hawk-like, in a blissful ease.

MARMALADE

MARMALADE appears to issue from melimelum, the honey-apple. The earliest marmalade was usually made of quinces. A seventeenth-century traveller, driving from Cambridge to London, took with him macaroons, marmalade (quince) and wine, which suggests a sweet tooth and a sticky meal on the road. The same gentleman's accounts show further fellowship of marmalade and sweet-cakes. Marmalade could be made of every fruit. Cherry marmalade was the old form of our (too rare) cherry jam. In the eighteenth century a Marmalade Madam was another name for a strumpet. *The London Spy*, who spelled them Marmulets, named them so. The word could also be an adjective and applied to the human heart, signifying soft and sweet. But now it has become limited in range to the conserve made of oranges or lemons. A pity. A Marmalade Madam, whose heart was by no means marmalade, strongly suggests a relentless daughter of the game with an eye to all her chances.

MARTINET

WITH its martial beginning Martinet strikes one as a fit, ferocious word, its moustaches bristling, its field-boots perfectly polished. Why Martinet? The familiar explanation is to discover (or imagine) a General of that family, noted for his peremptory style of giving orders and subsequent execution of discipline. This Martinet was supposed to be a Frenchman of Louis Quatorze period. But, browsing in the Rev. W. L. Blackley's *Word Gossip* (1869), I find this attribution vigorously rejected. Blackley wrote:

> Another illustration of the error of deducing words from individual or imagined names appears in the explanation commonly given of the word 'martinet'. It signifies in English a vexatiously strict commanding officer, and is altogether a military term. It is therefore alleged to be the name of some departed colonel named Martinet, who has thus for ever stamped the name he bore upon the character he gained. But 'martinet' in the Swiss superstition means the spirit of mischief, the malicious sprite, the bugbear, and in this sense, is mentioned by Victor Hugo (*Toilers of the Sea*, Vol. I) when setting forth how every country has at least its tradition of some such ill-conditioned Loki. And a special reason why such a Swiss word should have this extensive military sense to-day may be found in the fact that for so many centuries and in so many countries Swiss mercenaries formed a part of almost every European army.

Well, whichever way we have it, the word is right for its matter. You can almost hear it clicking its heels.

METEOR

COLONEL WALTER ELLIOT, writing an article with a
title drawn from Thomas Campbell's phrase 'The Meteor Flag of
England', once pointed out that England is still regarded as a
terrible and consuming force by some Scots and Welsh as well as
by many others further off: he also reminded us, incidentally, that
Campbell could flash into poetry as well as perform like an apt
rhetorician in the more belligerent types of verse. Meteors splutter
and blaze across the skies of art as well as of reality, but Campbell's
success was in making meteor an adjective.

> The meteor flag of England
> Shall yet terrific burn,
> Till danger's troubled night depart
> And the star of peace return.

The second couplet is ordinary enough, but the first does powerfully strike a light. The idea of the English or British flag as a fire-
ball which creates light and heat wherever it goes has the strength
of fancy proper to genuine poetry. The English, as Walter Elliot
insisted, have long come to regard themselves as lambs, meek and
sparkless, but the outer world, or at least a good deal of it, still
imagines British power to be a flambeau, incendiary bomb, or even
an engine of rocketing conspiracy. (At the time Elliot wrote a
prominent American paper was encouraging its readers to believe
that the dastardly scheme of Rhodes Scholarships was a vile plot
to capture, convert, and Anglicize decent, but innocent, young
Americans.) That is the mood which sees the Union Jack to be as
much a thing of fiery menace as any 'exhalations whizzing in
the air'. Campbell was sometimes inspired. His ode on the
'Pleasures of Hope' fell not so far behind Gray in quotability:

> Hope for a season bade the world farewell,
> And Freedom shrieked — as Kosciusko fell!

It was Campbell, not Gray, who noted,

> 'Tis distance lends enchantment to the view
> And robes the mountain in its azure hue.

The second line slid away, typically, for Campbell was not a stayer. His poetry came with a meteor flash. And when he fell, how deep the plunge!

> One moment may with bliss repay
> Unnumbered hours of pain,

So far, so decently obvious; but there followed,

> Such was the throb and mutual sob
> Of the knight embracing Jane.

Here, indeed, was a meteor absurdity.

MIZZLE

' I T was a murky October day that the hero of our tale, Mr. Sponge, or Soapey Sponge, as his good-natured friends called him, was seen mizzling along Oxford Street, winding his way to the West.' Mizzling, here, is disappearing: at least so the dictionaries say. But can a man be seen vanishing? Well, he can be seen about to vanish, fading out, and perhaps that is what Surtees had in mind. To me mizzling seems a good term for sauntering, moving slowly like the kind of rain that is called mizzling.

Mizzle, incidentally, is a word with a rich number of meanings. It is a very old variant of drizzle. 'Now 'gynnes to mizzle, hye we homeward fast' is Spenser's precautionary advice — to potential rheumatoids? To mizzle is also to confuse. The ancient sot was mizzled with his wine. It can be an alternative to muzzle. As a noun it is a form of measles, and so a child can be 'mizzled', i.e. covered with spots. These usages are mostly scarce and antique or a piece of local dialect. But in one sense or another the word hangs on and does not, like Soapey, go mizzling out of sight.

MORT

WILLIAM HARRISON in his *Description of England* (1587)
observed, on the subject of rogues and vagabonds, that a gentleman
called Thomas Harman had listed twenty-three species of this 'un-
gracious rabble'. Here is Harman's catalogue of idlers and 'nips':—

The several disorders and degrees amongst our idle vagabonds.

1.	Rufflers	2.	Uprightmen
3.	Hookers or anglers	4.	Rogues
5.	Wild Rogues	6.	Priggers of prancers
7.	Palliards	8.	Fraters
9.	Abrams	10.	Freshwater mariners or whipjacks
11.	Dummerers	12.	Drunken tinkers
13.	Swadders or pedlars	14.	Jarkmen or patricoes

Of the women kind.

1.	Demanders for glimmer or fire	2.	Bawdy-baskets
3.	Morts	4.	Autem morts
5.	Walking morts	6.	Doxies
7.	Dells	8.	Kinching morts
		9.	Kinching coes

Dover Wilson quotes this in his *Life in Shakespeare's England*
and adds some interpretations. The ruffler was a pretending rogue,
claiming service in the wars and showing as an honourable scar the
cicatrice of a tavern brawl. Uprightmen were top-rankers in
roguery. Hookers and anglers carried a staff with a hook in reserve,
with which they lifted desirable articles. Priggers of prancers were
horse-thieves; palliards were beggars in patched cloaks. Abrams
pretended madness in order to raise alms (Edgar's device in *King
Lear* would put him in this class, easily recognizable by an Elizabethan audience), Fraters were fraudulent collectors for charity,
freshwater mariners were bogus sailors, dummerers pretended to be

95

dumb, and jarkmen or patricoes were sham-clergy offering false marriages. Patrico is Pater Cove.

Now, by-passing the nicely entitled bawdy-baskets, we arrive at the morts. Why mort became a term for a girl nobody seems to know. A walking mort was a female vagabond, autem morts were married, Dells were virgins, and doxies were morts neither married nor virgin. Kinching morts would now be less picturesquely called 'juvenile delinquents, female'. Kinching coes are the same, masculline. Kinching is the equivalent of the German kinder or kindchen. The term lived on in English thieves' cant and Fagin's London knew the kinching-lay, i.e. the robbing of children sent out on errands. Demanders for glimmer or fire are described as false claimants to fire losses. But might not they also be people asking for a light or warmth (and light and warmth were not so easily come by in those days) and then stealing from their benefactors?

It is a formidable list and many of the terms have lived on. Mort seems to me the strangest; it is such a deathly name for a lively young party. Flagitious as the mort may have been, at least she was not likely to be at death's door, slow, crippled and cadaverous.

MUMBLE AND MAMMOCK

M U M B L E in the older sense of mouthing food softly seems worth rescue. A nasty old man who mumbles his food suggests a vivid picture of the toothless gums and futile striving after mastication. The verb was fairly common in the seventeenth and eighteenth centuries. Pope has it of dogs trained not to damage the shot bird. In his superb denunciation of 'Sporus' (Lord Hervey) he snaps:

> Yet let me flap this bug with gilded wings,
> This painted child of dirt, that stinks and stings,
> Whose buzz the witty and the fair annoys,
> Yet wit ne'er tastes, and beauty ne'er enjoys:
> So well-bred spaniels civilly delight
> In mumbling of the game they dare not bite.

A. L. Rowse in a poem about Cornwall, the dark woods of Duporth in particular, has these lines:

> Somewhere in the domed sky a gull laughs
> Above the turning world, and with shrill mirth
> That the sea should mumble the corners of the earth.

Another odd and picturesque word for eat was famble, which meant mouth without appetite. I have heard of mumble still used by English countrymen for eat without relish.

The opposite of mumble in this connection was mammock, which meant to tear greedily at one's prey or food. In Shakespeare's not very pleasing description of Coriolanus Junior, the 'very pretty boy with a confirmed countenance', it is told how he played, as it were, cat and mouse with a gilded butterfly, tumbling in his chase, until he grabbed the pretty thing. 'Whether his fall enraged him, or how 'twas, he did so set his teeth and tear it: oh, I warrant how he mammocked it.' At this point his mother protests that the lad is not 'a noble child', but 'a crack', which was Tudor-English for a 'bold, unbiddable boy'. Most of us will agree. Children mammocking butterflies seem at least as ugly a spectacle as old men mumbling chops: but both usages are mordant and are worth remembering. In July 1944, Bernard Shaw wrote a letter to *The Times* on the subject of small children and their proper treatment. He spoke of mothers mammocking their children as though it meant fondling in a motherly way. I could find no Dictionary support for this. Contrasting Irish individualism with German institutional efficiency, in the training of infants, G.B.S. wrote that in 'Connemara the mothers hugged them, mammocked them, kissed them, smacked them, talked baby talk to them or scolded them, in short maternally massaged them to their hearts' content'. Obviously Shaw did not wish to imply by his use of mammock the presence of domestic cannibalism in Connemara.

EDWARD THOMPSON has sung:

> Tramboon and cinnamon:
> Myrrh and myrabalon:
> Tamarind: olibanum:
> Civet and cardamum:

This from the beginning of a gorgeously aromatic, as well as resonant, poem called 'Bills of Lading'; its theme is the instruction once given by the Honourable East India Company to all Master Mariners. 'We look that our vessels, ere launched on the seas from Ind to Mozambique, be loaden with these.' Then follows a torrent of magnificent spices, herbs, condiments, cloths and Oriental kick-shaws of all kinds. Myrabalon, which sounds like a Babylonian miracle, some fruity masterpiece of the Hanging Gardens, is a species of plum. But what are

> Adatas and nassapores:
> Newries and cocatores:
> Percalloes and kastapores:
> Gurrahs and balasores:
> Calamdanes and scrutores?

Again there are listed,

> Hornes of rhenosseries
> Chaubletts and romaulees:
> Soosees: wax of bees:
> Harital and patanees.

Catalogue-poetry of this kind has always been enjoyed by lovers of a good noise since rhythm and rhyming began. It can be done with place-names (Edward Thomas was a master of that map-work), with flowers and herbs (Kipling and Sir Osbert Sitwell pre-eminent), or with Oriental cargoes (Masefield, Flecker, and

Thompson commanding). The glorious word-waterfall that is 'Bills of Lading' can be found in Thompson's *One Hundred Poems*, a little book containing specimens of a lifetime's utterance in many moods by a voice insufficiently heard and acknowledged.

NARD

NARD, or, more handsomely spikenard, has sacred significance, since, in Wyclif's words, 'Marie took a pound of oynement Spike-nard, or trewe nard, precious . . .' for her offering in the incident related by St. John. Nard is properly an aromatic balsam from a plant of that same name, but also means the balsam and aroma of any wood, especially the scent coming off a good log-fire. So it occurs in what seems to me one of the most exquisite of English lyrics, this of Ben Jonson:

> Have you seen but a bright lily grow
>   Before rude hands have toucht it?
> Have you markt but the fall of the snow
>   Before the soil hath smutcht it?
> Have you felt the wool of beaver,
>   Or swan's down ever?
> Or have smelt o' the bud o' the brier,
>   Or the nard in the fire?
> Or have tasted the bag of the bee?
> O so white, O so soft, O so sweet is she!

Jonson's place in letters has been curious. He was the god of his own day, regarded much above Shakespeare, yet is rarely acted now and that only in the case of two plays, *Volpone* and *The Alchemist*. I cannot remember the 'Old Vic' ever playing Jonson. Now we find the Jonsonian drama, in general, rather heavy, too allusive and learned, closely of its period, missing the perennial and universal appeal of Shakespeare. But the sometimes heavy-handed Ben had beautiful lightness in his lyrics, as the quoted stanza shows. For colour, too, he could rival Shakespeare in evoking the melancholy shade of sad cypress and the plaint of dark, sepulchral things. There are, for example, the lines beginning, with such superb lamentation and such a masterly and monosyllabic tattoo upon the noble drums of grief:

> Slow, slow, fresh fount, keep time with my salt tears,

It ends:

> Droop herbs and flowers,
> Fall grief in showers,
> Our beauties are not ours.
> O, I could still,
> Like melting snow upon some craggy hill,
> Drop, drop, drop, drop,
> Since Nature's pride is now a withered daffodil.

We have wandered from nard, but what matter? All great poetry has its own aroma, the nard of the divine fire, 'trewe nard, precious'.

NECKIT

N E C K has to be sadly mentioned as a case where English totally fails to hit the handsome mark. Are not the necks of ladies, as of swans, a main portion of their beauty? But what a mean, gritty, petty monosyllable we offer them! I was reminded of this by the second, and scarcely felicitous, verse of Douglas's dirge of 'Anne Laurie' which has too much haunted Scottish balladry since he composed its dulcet melancholy.

> She's bristit like a peacocke,
> She's neckit like a swan,
> She's jimp about the middle,
> Her waist ye weel might span.

Of jimp, a nice word, I wrote before. But neck and neckit? Do they at all suit that slender piece of woman which in the Song of Songs is a tower of ivory reaching up to the lips that are a scarlet thread? Drummond of Hawthornden tried hard in his madrigal,

> Like the Idalian Queen
> Her hair about her eyne,
> With neck and breast's ripe apples to be seen.

But neck remains obstinately with the mutton, madrigal or no madrigal. It is more of the butcher's shop than the beauty parlour. Its abuse as a verb, in slang, for cuddle and kiss is therefore the less regrettable.

PARSNIP

'FINE words butter no parsnips', we are told. But is parsnip itself a fine word? Scarcely. But an odd one and more amusing and attractive than the sickly article it represents — sickly, at any rate, to quite a number of palates including my own. The learned opine that parsnip comes from the Latin *pastinaca* and has attracted to itself the 'neep' or 'nip' found in turnip. The queer-sounding parsnip is 'a biennial umbelliferous plant with pinnate leaves and a pale yellow root'. This root has a sweetish flavour very different from the comparatively astringent tang of the turnip. Parsnip-haters have been long established in the land. In the scene of the play on *Sir Thomas More*, some of which has been attributed to Shakespeare's hand and handwriting, some remarks are passed on this theme during a popular discussion (strangely modern) on the influence of Immigrant Aliens. It is complained of these by one Lincoln that 'they eat more in our country than they do in their own' and also that they 'bring in strange roots, which is merely to the undoing of poor 'prentices, for what's a sorry parsnip to a good heart?'

Then one Williamson joins in the abuse of parsnips. 'Trash, trash. They breed sore eyes, and 'tis enough to infect the City with the palsy.' To this Lincoln replies, 'Nay, it has infected it with the palsy, for these bastards of dung, (as you know, they grow in dung) have infected us and it is our infection will make the City shake, which partly comes through the eating of parsnips'. Whether the sense be good enough for Shakespeare can hardly be settled by re-course to these few lines: certainly More's final speech, in defence of receiving aliens, is one of high and courteous sentiment and quite possibly of Shakespearean phrase.

The proverb about fine words buttering no parsnips is also un-complimentary to that root, which has ever lacked friends. Sir Walter Scott, in *The Legend of Montrose*, mentions the proverb as Southern and Stevenson in his *Book of Quotations* traces it back to the text of a play called *The Citizen* by the eighteenth-century dramatist Arthur Murphy. Wycherley in *The Plain Dealer* had it that 'fine words butter no cabbage'. Parsnips, buttered or plain, may just, I think, be permitted to fill a corner of the stew, if better things be scarce. The trouble is that, once set, they may grow all too generously: the idea that they need a deal of manure is by no means my own experience.

PASSIONAL

A PASSIONAL was a book relating the sufferings of Saints and Martyrs and ordered to be read on the days sacred to them. The word can also be an adjective and was so used with aphrodisiac significance in this astounding quatrain on the familiar theme of the fourth month and its genial influence.

> The April winds are magical
>   And thrill our tuneful frames,
> The garden-walks are passional
>   To bachelors and dames.

The author was Emerson.

PELTING

How many of the young who are dragged through John of Gaunt's speech on this other Eden, demi-Paradise, blessed plot, happy breed, etc., could define the pelting farm which he mentions? One might imagine it to be a holding where pelts or skins are obtained, a sheep-farm. (Silver-fox-farmers are servants of luxury, then, of course, unknown.) But pelting was an ancient and rather pleasing epithet for small, trashy, worthless. It is much the same as paltry, which probably has the same origin in palt, an old Scandinavian word for bits and pieces, dross. Shakespeare applied pelting to small streams, small farms, small villages, and petty officers; the last must not be understood in our naval sense. Pelting and paltry are both nicely dismissive adjectives. The very sound of them humiliates the noun to which they are attached. A pelting farm is obviously a hovel with some weedy acres, while a pelting petty officer must be a contemptible little Jack-in-office. It seems a pity that pelting should have lost favour; and paltry, too, is a trifle literary now. We have our own terms of derision in common use for pelting people and paltry things — terms which may be ruder. But are they really more apt and effective?

PERJINK AND OTHERS

I said in the introduction to this book that I had been scolded for introducing too many Scottish words into previous volumes. I gave my reason for neglecting these scoldings and now propose to support that argument by introducing here a whole parcel of Scottish words. Anti-Caledonians are at full liberty, and are even advised, to practise the art of skipping for a page or so. It was observed by Henry Fielding's Jonathan Wild that many men fail in wickedness for want of going deep enough in, a remark which seems to me, as my experience of life grows with the years, to be both accurate in fact and profound in principle. (It certainly does not apply, however, to such as Hitler.) Accordingly, if it be a trespass to pick a few of Scotland's verbal bluebells or king-thistles, I shall not commit the further error of self-limitation to one or two such blooms. Let there be no meagre paddling in the Lallans burn, but a full plunge into that pool of peaty waters. All this arises from a passage in a lecture on 'The Scottish Character as it was viewed by Scottish authors from Galt to Barrie', delivered by Mr. James Bridie to the Greenock Philosophical Society and reprinted in his rich volume of assorted sweets and bitters called *Tedious and Brief*. I quote this at length and with no more permission than a consenting silence on the author's part.

The Scot, on the other hand, has always taken an almost morbid delight in oddities of mind or behaviour. A remarkable proportion of his vocabulary consists of words which are lightning caricatures of 'character' seen from this aspect. In any railway carriage he can mark his fellow passengers as gaucie, menseful, forfochen, couthie, perjink, cappernoytit, fusionless, dour or douce. It is interesting to reflect what a large proportion of this vocabulary describes character in which mental defect is a prominent feature. The Scots conversation is full of thowless, bloutering nyaffs; of feckless, donnart, doited, havering gowks; of daft, glaikit, foutering tawpies; of snuitit gomerals. Next to the Idiot come the Slut and the Harridan. It would be a mistake to stress this too much. A nation which makes a thorough study of character in its most subtle forms must necessarily be rich in terms of abuse. Much the most effective kind of abuse is the intimate and personal. To call a man a blackguard gives him such a wide range of choice that the sting is dissipated. But, if you call him a rowting sump or a wullie-wallocks and are careful in your choice of epithet, you hold, as 'twere, a mirror up to his defect; you get home.

Apart from the language of denigration, there is plenty in the Scottish tongue to show that here is a race that takes character seriously and has an endless variety to choose from.

What applied to the race in general, applied to Scottish writers in particular.

As an absentee Scot, I must confess to some weakness in the finer shades of the Doric, Lallans, Scots, or what you will. The words for fool seemed to explain themselves, but the previous list of adjectives needed interpretation to be fully relished. I consulted Mr. Bridie, who replied with the natural courtesy of a Lowland Scot and a punctuality most unusual in gentlemen of the artistic professions. Here are his definitions, described as 'not official, but the connotations I have heard commonly employed'.

Gawcie (or gaucie): 'Handsome' is only part of it. It means also jolly, 'well-put-on', flourishing, euphoric, buxom (if it applies to a woman). It implies a large and jovial sort of grace . . . like a chrysanthemum or a dahlia.

Menseful: Thoughtful. Not so much sicklied over with the pale cast as intelligent and considerate and considering.

Forfochen: Thoroughly depressed. Also implying the battered effect produced by Fortune's buffets, and a tendency to lamentations.

Couthie: Comfortable. Neat. Well-to-do. Opposite of 'uncouth'. An old meaning is popular or kenspeckle.

Perjink: Tidy. Pernicketty. Precise.

Fusionless: Sapless. Feeble. Without fusion of the elements.

Cappernoytit: Confused chronically in the intellects. Slightly deranged. This is odd, because *Capernoity* means a mischief-making gossip. *Cabair*, a babbler; *naitheas*, mischief. It is an adjective, of course, in both cases.

Dour: Same as 'dur'. Hard, obstinate, glum, grim.

Douce: Gentle, courteous. Also implies that the douce person never gets rattled.

Glaikit: From *gleogach*, silly. Applied very often to an idiotic appearance, rather than to habits. Burns uses both above words in 'The Unco Guid':

> That frequent pass douce Wisdom's door
> For glaikit folly's portals.

Sumph: Is the right spelling, I think. A heavy, dull, stupid person.

Wullie-Wallocks: An effeminate boy. Also implies silliness.

The allusion to the spelling of sumph was caused by my protesting against Bridie's sump. The latter is a drain. The former, as I remember from boyhood talk in Scotland, is a dolt. 'A muckle sumph' was supposed to be finally dismissive of a person's claims to any grey matter.

The fusion in fusionless is really the same as Shakespeare's foison, which means the sap or strength of a plant or crop, leading to plenty in the field and larder.

Certainly it is a fine list of what Armado called the congruent epitheton. Apply it, for example, to Hamlet. Angered by his gawcies mother's second marriage, the douce and menseful prince turns dour and forfochen, and rails at himself for being fusionless. For safety's sake he pretends to be glaikit, no dull sumph but certainly capper noytit. He kills the perjink Polonius and is brought a challenge by the wullie-wallocks Osric. So life in Elsinore is scarcely couthie.

Would English be the worse for borrowing from Scottish? Am I really to be scolded?

PHIZ

P H Y S I O G N O M Y means the study of outlines or faces, but soon, even as early as the seventeenth century, it came to signify the face itself. Being accustomed to phiz, or phizog, as a rather poor nineteenth-century joke (phiz was used thus even earlier), I was surprised to find the full word used in sacred circumstances by William Strode, the Caroline poet, in his lines on Fairford Church and its famous windows. Contrasting the stained glass portraits with visages in a looking glass he says,

> But these have holy physnomy:
> Each pane instructs the Laity
> With silent eloquence: for here
> Devotion leads the eye, not eare,

To note the catechising paynt,
Whose easy phrase doth so acquaint
Our sense with Gospell that the Creede
In such a hand the weake may reade:
Such types even yet of vertue bee,
And Christ, as in a glass, wee see.

The catechizing paint means the instructing paint. Catechize now means rather to ply with questions than to inform through query and answer; to Strode obviously the catechist was a teacher, not an examiner.

PHONEY

THIS strange term of contempt and dismissal has spread powerfully from America and has almost ousted the once fashionable bogus from usage over here. Bogus, which may have some link with bogy, was an earlier importation from the west. Phoney is usually spelt thus and not with an 'f', suggesting some connection with telephony. But why should a telephoned message be more false or pretentious than a written one? The only explanation of phoney in my acquaintance, is that given by Eric Partridge in his *Dictionary of R.A.F. Slang*. Commenting on the various kinds of 'gen' (see note on 'intelligence') he considers 'phoney gen' (doubtful information) and concludes 'Phoney from the American underworld, which adapted it from Fawney, the English underworld term for a ring, the transition being effected by "Brum" jewellery'. The *O.E.D.* gives fawney as a brass ring disposed of as gold. Any other theories? No doubt the victory of phoney owes something to the sound of the word. But why the 'ph'? It is true that such words as fair and famous begin with 'f', but the 'f' sound is frequently contemptuous. Filthy, feeble, fatuous, futile, fiddling, finicky, fatheads and fools are just the folk to be fobbed off with faked and phoney articles. It is unquestionable that phoney is expressive and comes easily off the curling lip.

PICCADILLA

I T had numerous spellings, as did so many people and things of Tudor times. It meant the cut-work of the great Tudor collar: then the collar itself, the vast neck-piece of fashion and display. Excessive people exceeded in their piccadills.

> Her Piccadill above her crowne upreares:
> Her Fardingale is set above her eares.

And so to Piccadilla Hall, a mansion built in the late sixteenth century somewhere near Piccadilly Circus. Why the name? Two answers are usually given. One, that the area was then the fringe or necklet of the town, which still hugged the river between Westminster and the City. Two, that Piccadilla Hall was the seat of a jumped-up clothier, who had sold the modish article at high profit; the town thus gave the nick-name to all his demesne. Some say the name of the Piccadill-king was Baker; others say Higgins. There is a story that he bought an acre and a half for fifty pounds, on the whole, and in the light of the centuries, a good speculation. So the name was there and the great herbalist of the time could write, 'The small wild buglosse grows upon the drie ditch bankes about Pickadilla'. Charles II endeavoured to honour his Queen by calling the road, leading west from Piccadilla Hall, Portugal-street. But this pleased neither London pride nor Cockney instinct. The public insisted on having its Piccadilly, and that name became 'Official' during the middle of the eighteenth century.

The voice of the people was certainly in this case the voice of understanding. Piccadilly was a nice invention. The title of Pall Mall to the south started with a courtly game, but suitably began to signify later on the saunterings of those whose day's occupation was to move from Foodle's Club to Poodle's, there to find a new audience for their observations on the Government and the decay of the nation. Piccadilly was obviously a lighter street, gayer, less heavily fortified with red leather armchairs, less garrisoned by those club servants for whom no adjective but 'august' will suffice.

It mingled expense with taste, clothes and caviare with books and pictures, and all with delight. Invitations to go down the Strand have been the cry of the pleasuring Londoner, but Piccadilly is a senior claimant for convivial honours. It became, with its absurd syllables, the centre of the traveller's dream of home. A. H. Clough, abroad, idealized even the paving-stones on which our feet have burned and ached on summer days:

> Oh, you flags of Piccadilly,
> Though I hated you, I vow
> I could wish with all my heart
> You were underneath me now.

So the old Tudor collar survives the centuries — and not in London only. Other cities have liked the queer road-name and adopted it.

POMPION

COSTARD of *Love's Labour Lost*, one of Shakespeare's earliest and most likeable clowns, took the part of Pompey in the masquerade of the Nine Worthies. He called the great one Pompion. An audience of the 1590's was more likely than an audience of to-day to see a jest here, Pompion being of old a pumpkin. The joke is a small enough matter, but the word has quality and goes marching and singing fitly with the other flowers and herbs which end with -ion. It brings up the rear of good floral and vegetable company in the Sitwellian lines of 'Winter the Huntsman':

> Then through marine groves slowly brushes
> Old Deborah the herbalist,
> To pick a thousand verdigris grasses
>   — The evening dew her alchemist —,
> Looking for eglantine,
> Columbine, celandine,
> Wolfsbane and oxbane,
> Sainfoin and fluellin,

Wortdragon, snapdragon,
Martagon, campion,
Tarragon, rampion,
Rocambole, pompion.

Rocambole looks handsome and rolls majestically upon the ear. It has, perhaps, less dignity, though much utility, in the larder, being 'a species of leek indigenous to Northern Europe, used as a seasoning for dishes; Spanish garlic; sand-leek'.

Pompion has become pumpion in *The Merry Wives*. 'We'll use this unwholesome humidity, this gross, watery pumpion', says Mistress Ford of Falstaff.

POTWALLOPER

A CORRESPONDENT following up my previous note on wallop, asks me to define and explain 'potwalloper'. Well, I can do no more than quote Chambers, who thus expounds the mystery. For him a pot-walloper is 'A pot-boiler, a voter in certain English boroughs, where, before the Reform Bill of 1832, everyone who boiled a pot, i.e. every male householder or lodger, was entitled to a vote'. Why the 'walloper'? From old English *Weallan*, to boil. Presumably the pot-waller or pot-walloper was regarded, in the corrupt state of the Reform politics, as almost certainly a dishonest fellow. At any rate pot-walloper became a term of contempt and abuse. Pot-boiling (complimentary in the Book of Job, 'He maketh the deep to boil like a pot') has been a derogatory term among literary folk for more than a century. It means to turn out routine stuff for the money it brings in. It is curious that authors should have foregone the more vigorous and picturesque term. How agreeable for one scribe to dismiss another as a potwalloping hack!

Pot-walloper has nothing to do with swallowing pots of 'wallop', i.e. mild beer, but it would be a good enough term for a human fixture at 'the local'.

PRANG AND PRUNE

THE R.A.F.'s use of prang for crash, smash, or otherwise mess up has no discoverable basis in verbal tradition. Anything can be pranged, from the largest bomber to a date with Jane. Chief prangers are prunes; these are simpletons or mutts. Here, too, there is no excuse to be found in the dictionary for attaching to folly the fruit of 'Prunus Domestica'. Why should a plum be the symbol of a prize and the prune signify only a booby? There is no justice in these things. Prunes, doubtless, began to come down in the world when they were first associated with demure speech and the petty gentility that goes with it. The 'prunes and prism' style of diction is at least as old as Dickens, who associated the two words, and became the accepted contrast with frank, vigorous speech. So the comic curates of conventional farce in Victorian times (we have ceased to titter at curates now that so many of them are Rugby Football Internationals or champions of the boxing ring) came into the sphere of prunery because of their prunes-and-prism enunciation. At least, that seems the likeliest origin for the airman's use of prune. Pilot Officer Prune became almost an official figure of fun, the example of what every man with wings should never be, a pranger of all and sundry prangable things.

PRESENTLY

WHAT greater tribute could there be to the human instinct for delay than the swing of meaning in presently? What was a pressing and urgent word for now ('Go presently' is a brisk, immediate command in Shakespeare) to-day simply means soon, later on, almost any time. The Scots, a punctual folk, have, it seems, to some extent retained the proper use of presently. The kind of Scot who uses presently for now might also use continue for put off. This, too, is a word employable for two quite contrary purposes. We are accustomed to continue an action in the sense of plodding on.

But it was possible in Scotland and was once possible in England too (and still is in legal language) to continue in the sense of knocking off or adjourning. A correspondent has sent me a tale of a Scottish Chairman of an English Council who, when wearied by too much talk of the disputatious, would say, 'Gentlemen, do you not think it would be well to continue the debate?' The argumentative assenting gladly, he would answer, 'Then the debate is continued until the next meeting' and either rise or proceed to other business.

It is certainly odd that 'We shall presently continue' can even now, with a little admixture of Scots, legal English and ordinary English, mean four quite different things, e.g. (1) We shall immediately carry on. (2) We shall carry on later on. (3) We shall immediately adjourn. (4) We shall adjourn later on.

PRIME

PRIME can be a verb meaning fill or charge or a noun with a special significance in fencing. Usually it is an adjective and one of strangely limited employment. It has been commonly applied to one kind of Minister, many kinds of meat, and certain kinds of mover. It used to be the butcher's darling, adorning and commending the steaks beside the market naphtha-flare or pinned upon the massed mutton of the Flesher's Saturday Night, with limbs set 'steadily shoulder to shoulder' — like the Boys of the Old Brigade — or legs all in order — as in a troupe of dancing girls. It is odd how certain trades annex certain epithets. Prime has long been the prime favourite of British butchery.

Then there is 'in the prime', as applied to the lives of men and women. Gordon Hewart, late Lord Chief Justice, once defined this prime as the age of fifty-five. This was consolation to many and would have staggered an Elizabethan who regarded two-score as an age of wrinkled ruin. (Shakespeare, who talked frequently of youth's sweet prime, was jostled by a rough wind in May into brooding over summer as a tenant shortly to be evicted and was likewise set aghast by the siege of forty winters, digging deep trenches in the brow.) Mr. Shaw, on the other hand, as a good Methuselist, has put 'the prime' away up in the centuries and is properly living up to his own prescription. There is ugly use of prime for lecherous in *Othello*: 'Were they as prime as goats.' But mostly prime rides in good company, with the leading citizen, the sweet of the year, and the best of the carcass. Do vegetarians answer prime beef with 'prime cabbages'? I think not.

PUISNE

How many know that a Puisne Judge, who sounds so imposing, is, in fact, only a puny one? Puisne is puis-né, later-born, therefore junior, inferior, and so, at last, feeble. A puny boy ought to mean a youngster, not a weakling, but the word is now commonly twisted to the latter sense. Puisne remains legal English or Anglicized French and it appears for junior of the bar in a holiday poem of Thomas Randolph's,

> Come, spur away,
>   I have no patience for a longer stay,
> But must go down
>   And leave the chargeable noise of this great town:
> I will the country see
> Where old Simplicity
> Though hid in gray, doth look more gay
> Than Foppery in plush and scarlet clad.

He adds,

> More of my days
> I will not spend to gain an idiot's praise
> Or to make sport
> For some slight puisne of the Inns of Court.

It is interesting to find here the old use of chargeable, which means simply burdensome; later on it came to mean as a rule liable to legal process and lost its other significance. But chargeable lingers in Biblical English rather as Randolph used it for burdensome. David feared that he and his sons might be chargeable or burdensome to Absalom during a visit, much as King Lear's hundred knights became most chargeable to Goneril and Regan. That acute Shakespearean of Cambridge George Rylands once amusingly suggested the production of *King Lear* with scores of the lustiest and hungriest undergraduates following Lear round on his visits, just to show what the ladies and their larders had to suffer. In short, he would rally for the King a chargeable crowd — and far from puisne.

PURL and WIMPLE

THE language of running water is, as it should be, liquid, effervescent, and picturesque. The men of the north chose 'force' for a water-fall and this dynamic monosyllable seems perfect. But the dictionaries refer it back to foss and one must salute their learning. Foss, however, was only a ditch. Is the majesty of High Force, in Teesdale, England's greatest water-fall, superb itself and nobly placed, merely ditch-like? Surely it is forceful. We can leave it, along with its finely titled and no less impressive neighbour Cauldron Snout and all the Forces of Cumbria, to hurl their grandeur down the fells and the years. Let us turn to gentler matters, i.e. to the purlers and dimplers and wimplers.

Purling streams bring their music to most parties given by the Nature Poets. The Caroline Cartwright uses purling in his beautiful,

> Seal up her eyes, O Sleep, but flow
> Mild as her manners, to and fro;
> Slide soft into her, that yet she
> May receive no wound from thee.
> And ye present her thoughts, O dreams,
> With hushing winds and purling streams
> Whiles hovering silence sits without,
> Careful to keep disturbance out.

The Augustans liked their rills to be purlers and Pope, in his pastoral vein, made great use of the word.

It has never been finally determined whether a purling stream is a melodious, a galloping, or just a trotting one. Purl, indeed, is a word of widely varying significance. It is a twisted thread (hence the knitter's purl) or a whirl of agitated waters. It has been used of beer infused with other liquors, usually gin. Of those licensed premises so strictly conducted by Miss Abbey Potterson, the Six Jolly Fellowship-Porters, Dickens wrote in *Our Mutual Friend*:

> For the rest, both the tap and parlour of the Six Jolly Fellowship-Porters gave upon the river, and had red curtains matching the noses of the regular customers, and were provided with comfortable fireside tin utensils, like models of sugar-loaf hats, made in that shape that they might, with their pointed ends, seek out for themselves glowing nooks in the depths of the red coals, when they mulled your ale, or heated for you those delectable drinks, Purl, Flip, and Dog's Nose. The first of these humming compounds was a speciality of the Porters, which, through an inscription on its door-posts, gently appealed to your feelings as 'The Early Purl House'. For, it would seem that Purl must always be taken early; though whether for any more distinctly stomachic reason than that, as the early bird catches the worm, so the early purl catches the customer, cannot here be resolved.

Is Purl a term ever used in taverns now? Certainly Dog's Nose abides.

Returning to the more temperate waters we find that a purl is an act of whirling. To purl, the verb, is to whirl or overthrow, especially to cast human beings to the ground. Hence 'to come a purler'. The purling of brooks is usually a gentle form of whirling. But many people would probably think of purl not as a motion but as a tranquil, murmurous sound, a pleasant plashing of the waters. Hardy's 'The purl of waters through the weirs' suggests ear-music to me, but to Clare purling was 'eye-music', if I may use a phrase of Wordsworth's ('the soft eye-music of slow-waving boughs').

Of a gravel-paved brook Clare wrote 'we often sat to see it purl along'. This makes a purling stream akin to a dimpling one.

> Eternal smiles their emptiness betray
> As shallow streams run dimpling all the way

is Pope's usage. The Scots have preferred wimple, which is possibly caused by the general association of 'w' with liquidity. If waters and waves are wet, why should they not wimple instead of dimple? A wimple means any kind of twisted thing as well as a folded head-dress. Tay and Tweed wimpled for Allan Ramsay,

> Nor those fair Straths that water'd are
> With Tay and Tweed's smooth Streams,
> Which gentily and daintily
> Eat down the flowery Braes
> As greatly and quately
> They wimple to the Seas.

The 'quately', which now seems the most odious specimen of 'refaned' Southern English, surprisingly turns up as good Edinburgh of 1728. 'Eat down the Braes' is odd and rather ugly. But 'wimple to the seas' is capital, especially to all who know the rivers mentioned. Burns do not wimple down the glen: their movement is too sharp and broken. Rivers wimple in straths, which are broader places of gentler fall. Tay, especially, wimples from Aberfeldy on to Perth.

QUARELET

A WORD of three syllables, denoting something cut from a quarrel, which was the old word for a quarry as well as the lasting word for a brawl; thereafter it meant any kind of stone or gem. Quarelet certainly is rare, but it comes up shining in Herrick,

> Some ask how pearls did grow
>   And where?
> Then spoke I to my girl
>   To part her lips and showed them there
>   The quarelets of pearl.

Pearl would seem to be the last kind of gem to be associated with quarrying; but let that pass. It is strange that so nice a word for stones and jewels should have slipped through the fingers of authors habitually eager for an attractive synonym.

QUINSY

A STRIKING word for a nasty business. It has been suggested to me that quinsy, a very painful and dangerous swelling in the throat, is connected with quince, 'a hard, acid, yellowish pear-shaped fruit' whose bitterness may have constrictive results. (Quinine is another matter, being an alkaloid product, both chemically and verbally, of cinchona.) The dictionaries do not link quinsy with quince, but attribute it to the Greek word for a dog-collar, cynanche. The Greek dog, cuon, has given us, then, both cynic, the philosopher who carried his contempt of worldly pleasure so far as to go and live in a tub or kennel, and quinsy, because a collar can be to a dog what an inflammation of the throat can be to man, namely a pain in the neck.

RAMP

To use the words ramp and racket for swindle is now so common that it is interesting to come across an early usage of a similar kind. The verb to ramp has long meant to steal or snatch as well as to rage, to be rampant and rampageous. I take it that steal is the meaning of ramp in this remarkable passage from John Marston's 'Antonio's Revenge', which I noticed in T. S. Eliot's Essay on Marston:

> The rawish dank of clumsy winter ramps
> The fluent summer's vein; and drizzling sleet
> Chilleth the wan bleak cheek of the numb'd earth,
> While snarling gusts nibble the juiceless leaves
> From the nak'd shuddering branch. . . .

Or does ramp here mean obstruct? The word ramper, something built up, almost a barrier, is sometimes used in the country for a ridge-built track or road. 'Fluent summer' fascinates too. Flowing with what? Sap and foison, as Shakespeare would have said, or just our usual holiday rain? Ramp, in Shakespeare, is a wanton wench. Iachimo talks of the daughters of the game as 'variable ramps'.

REACTIONARY

To call a man who disagrees with you a reactionary is extremely easy and extremely common. Reactionary — it is a nice, long, punishing word, like a series of slaps in the face. As words go, it is quite a youngster. Shakespeare, for example, would not have had the faintest notion what you meant by calling his Coriolanus a reactionary. Only in the nineteenth century did it begin to be used and now it is very familiar. You can hardly listen to or read any speech by a Left Wing politician without hearing his opponents called Reactionaries.

And yet, logically, the word could be applied to the Left just as much as to the Right. A reactionary is simply one who reacts. He used to be called Reactionist. He is one who, as the *Oxford Dictionary* defines him, displays some energy in response to a stimulus. Obviously we are all reacting to something all the time. We are all, to that extent, reactionaries. 'If you prick us, do we not bleed? If you tickle us, do we not laugh? If you wrong us, shall we not revenge?' Shylock's argument was of man's universality in reactions. This word reaction has been particularly popular lately to signify especially a response of mind. It is now fashionable to ask a person what is his reaction to this or that when all you mean is 'What do you think about this or that?' We live in a world of complex, fixation, and reaction. If you do anything so nice and normal as to love your mother, some learned ass will tell you that you have a maternal complex or a mother fixation. He will certainly use the word reaction when any ordinary person would say thought or opinion.

The reactionary man, then, is one who responds to some outside action or stimulus. How did it come to mean in politics a stickler for the old ways? It might just as well mean a stickler for the new ways, one responding or reacting to the need for reform. It is hard to say just how this twist of meaning came about. But the fact is there. Reactionary came to signify the man who reacts against change and sees ruin in what other people call progress. Once the word had got this meaning, of a rebel against alteration, it became the favourite weapon of every speaker demanding any sort of alteration. It may be an absurd word because a so-called reactionary may be so inert or so conversative as not to want any action of any kind. His response to stimulus is just to sit still. He merely wants tradition to continue, while he himself is left alone. To call that reaction might be to flatter it. But, in any case, reaction now has such a bad name that few Tories would like to be called by it. How many members of the Conservative Party would rise up and personally claim to be reactionary?

Politicians do enjoy this kind of loose labelling. It makes things so easy. It side-steps the need for clear thinking, and clear thinking is hard work. It rouses emotion easily.

The only hope of sensible politics lies in the ability and willingness of every man and woman to know and say what they mean by the terms they use. It is ridiculous to scream against reactionaries unless you are quite clear about what they are supposed to be reacting against. That, at least, is my own personal reaction.

It is amusing to collect a list of contrary and cancelling labels with their customary adjectives, as used by the political Right and Left. An article on 'Le Mot Juste' in the *Economist* (March 24th, 1945) collected some nice specimens to which I have added.

Left	Right
Planning	Regimentation
Out-worn creeds	Dangerous ideologies
Clamour of the panic-stricken rich	Timely protest of responsible men
Right to exploit	Freedom of the subject
Hard-faced men thinking only of their pockets	Provident citizens with a stake in the country
Stale shibboleths of a decaying capitalism	Traditional principles on which our national prosperity is built

What then of a vile reactionary? How do we translate him for the benefit of the Right? I suggest:

> A stout defender of all that is best in our glorious national heritage of character and commerce.

RIGADOON

SIR OSBERT SITWELL had a phrase of exotic inspiration in which all things lurid and livid took hands and danced in a fantastic ring.

> The Mexican dwarfs can dance for miles
> Stamping their feet and scattering smiles,
> Till the loud hills laugh and laugh again
> At the dancing dwarfs in the golden plain.

It is a world of flamingo and fandango, of all strange hues, shapes, rhythms, ecstasies.

> On the coast of Coromandel
> Dance they to the tunes of Handel,

and later

> Saraband and rigadoon
> Dance they through the purring noon.

Rigadoon, a glorious word, whatever the motion, may or may not have been Handel's idea of a dance, but it belonged to his century and was apparently named after its creator, M. Rigaud. Has there since been a Señor Rumba? I had imagined a Dancing Mistress in Blackpool called Madame Valeta as creatress and nominatress of that discreet fandango so popular in the Tower Ballroom. But no. A Yorkshire friend once announced to me decisively, 'It were a Le-uds man as invented Valeta'. No more to be said. It will be noted that Leeds had nearly honoured Malta's capital before Malta came to greater glory. I would like to hear a Blackpool Master of Ceremonies suddenly command his myriads to take partners or otherwise line up for 'Saraband and Rigadoon'. The Scots know about rigadoons. In their old song of Mally Lee,

A Prince came out frae 'mang them a', wi' garter at his knee,
And danced a stately rigadoon wi' bonnie Mally Lee.

The Sitwellian rigadoons sound less royal and refined.

RUDESBY

SHAKESPEARE twice uses 'rudesby' for rude fellow. Katharina
the Shrew cries out,

> I must forsooth be forc'd
> To give my hand, oppos'd against my heart
> Unto a mad-brain rudesby, full of spleen.

'Rudesby, be gone,' says Olivia to Sir Toby.

The employment of 'by' at the end of another word to give a
contemptuous, dismissive flavour is interesting and has in its time
made some pretty terms of depreciation. But the time is over now.
Fusby, for silly, fussy fellow, has become fuss-pot. Stephen Gosson
in his *Schoole of Abuse* (1579) used hangsby for a hanger-on.
Sneaksby we no longer see, nor idlesby either. Wigsby for a judge
or barrister or any perruqued person has also disappeared. Sneaksby,
by the way, is often associated in old writing with 'milksoppe and
meacocke'. The meacock, with or without e, is another casualty.
Of him Petruchio said,

> 'Tis a world to see
> How tame, when men and women are alone,
> A meacock wretch can make the curstest shrew.

He was, when alive and puling, a feeble, effeminate creature, the
obvious sport of a rudesby.

RUFFLE

ONE of the chief occupations of journalists in war-time is finding
polite names for set-backs and disasters. How well accustomed
readers everywhere must have grown to strategic retirements,
movements to pre-prepared positions, elasticity of defence, and

tactful regroupings on more favourable ground. While reading the history of Bonnie Prince Charlie's fatal campaign in 1745, I came across one of the most charming of these euphemisms. On the night of Culloden, Macleod, the Prince's aide-de-camp, wrote from Gortleg to Cluny MacPherson:

> Dear Sir,
> You have heard no doubt ere now of the ruffle we met this forenoon . . . Dispatch is the more necessary that His Highness has something in view which will make amends for this day's ruffle.

Well, there was no panic there. But ruffle! At least a thousand of the scanty Highlanders were dead and many were doomed to slaughter in the next few days. Of course there could be no 'amends for this day's ruffle'. The game was up and Charles Edward Stewart knew it: he could tell a ruffle from a rout. Brave in his own defeat and escapade, he never mustered the clans again. The ordinary ruffle is a disturbance or upset. It is gentle enough as a rule. The placid waters of the lake, the tranquil contents of the mind, these are the matters of berufflement. Ruffles of another kind once flowed round the neck or adorned a cavalier's boot-top. But ruffling, on the whole, is a tender process, far short of calamity, and has little in common with a Culloden. Amid all our admissions and mitigations of enforced retreat in 1940, no ingenious sub-editor ever thought of mentioning 'a ruffle in the Low Countries'.

SCRIMP AND SCRUMPTIOUS

IN a review which he wrote for *The Observer* A. L. Rowse used the word scrumptious to express his delight and excused himself for the choice of adjective by reference to the O.E.D. Consulting that high authority, I find that scrumptious is there given Dictionary Status and thus defined, 'Probably identical with the dialect scrimptious, mean, stingy, close-fisted, related to scrimption, a small quantity'. So scrumptious starts by meaning careful or fastidious, exacting, and then is applied to the things which fastidious gentlemen prefer. A blonde for example, not exacting or fastidious herself, might yet be scrumptious. I am inclined to disbelieve in this derivation by way of scrimption and to regard scrumptious as a word employed for praise because of its own simply and inescapably scrumptious sound; it is as full of enjoyment as a mouthful of strawberries and cream. Scrimp has been much used by the Scots as an adjective as well as verb:

> He gangs about sornan frae place to place
> As scrimp of Manners as of Sense and Grace,

sang Ramsay (To sorn is to go begging). Scrimp thus used is almost a scrumptious word.

SECURITY

W H A T a tyrant this word has been in our time! Security censored our letters and our news, condemned us to Stygian darkness, robbed us of sign-posts, maps, cameras. The word, incidentally, as a correspondent reminded me, has been a total traitor to itself, since in Latin and at first in English it meant without care, easeful, feckless. So Shakespeare had it several times. 'Page is an ass, a secure ass', said Ford. Hamlet Senior was murdered in his 'secure hour' — there we get the contradiction of meaning at its most extreme. Macbeth's witches also proclaimed doctrine once most odious to Mr. Herbert Morrison.

> And you all know, security
> Is mortals' chiefest enemy.

How then did the word swing round so much that a man's secure hour could really be his safe one? One can argue it out like a Shakespearean clown.

> 'And if a man be careless, then, argal, he must be free from care.' 'Ay, marry is he.' 'And if he be free from care, then he stands in no hazard, for danger is a care. So your careless man is one out of hazard and your secure man is your safe one!'

So security moves on from the risks caused by neglect to the immunity from risk caused by taking thought or even by being remote. Adonais in death was secure 'From the contagion of the world's slow stain'. 'Security be our watchword' cried the Elder Pitt. Shakespeare would hardly have understood that. Finally the word ends in the strong-box of the lawyer and the financiers as the very token of safety. And thence to the Home Office and all the engines and apparatus of hush-hushery. Did ever a term so stand upon its head?

SHALLOP

SHALLOP is a form of ancientry dear to Victorian poets and as much a piece of 'poetese' as palfrey. Indeed you can swear that Tennyson's Enid or Elaine must at one time have mounted a palfrey and ridden away to embark in a shallop. Tennyson doted on shallops. In an odd little poem called 'The Islet' he produced a minstrel singing,

> 'And shall it be over the seas
> With a crew that is neither rude nor rash,
> But a bevy of Eroses apple-cheek'd,
> In a shallop of crystal ivory-beak'd,
> With a satin sail of a ruby glow,
> To a sweet little Eden on earth that I know,
> A mountain islet pointed and peak'd;
> Waves on a diamond shingle dash,
> Cataract brooks to the ocean run,
> Fairily-delicate palaces shine
> Mixt with myrtle and clad with vine',

Obviously this is perfect shallop-country. When the G.B.S. of the eighteen-nineties wanted to portray a very poetical, hyper-aesthetical, foot-in-the-grave young man, he made him (Marchbanks in *Candida*) prate of shallops.

'A boat — a tiny shallop to sail away in, far from the world, where the marble floors are washed by the rain and dried by the sun: where

the south wind dusts the beautiful green and purple carpets. Or a chariot — to carry us up into the sky where the lamps are stars. . . .'
Justly may we decide that Eugene Marchbanks was not a major poet.

Plainly shallops in 'poetese' are very airy-fairy vessels. It is disconcerting therefore to discover that they are in lexicography just 'large, heavy boats with lug-sails'. In other words a shallop, or chaloupe, is the substantial French cousin of a solid Dutch sloop, but in poetry shallops are cockle-shell creations, elfin caravels, and ever more shall be so.

SILVERLING

A CHARMING name for a fish flashing its way through clear water. It occurs in a somewhat cryptic passage of Christopher Smart's 'Song to David', that remarkable precursor of Ralph Hodgson's 'Song of Honour'. After a verse about palms and jasmines in Adoration bound, Smart added,

> Increasing days their reign exalt,
> Nor in the pink and mottled vault
> The opposing spirits tilt;
> And, by the coasting raider spyed,
> The silverlings and crusians glide
> For ADORATION gilt.

All very mysterious! The pink and mottled vault with its jousting of contrary spirits suggests to me mainly the stomach of one who has seriously mixed his drinks. But the fifth line adds finely to the angler's lexicon. Crusians or crucians are perch or carp. Silverlings are sometimes shekels, but here some sort of gold-fish which happen to have the lighter gleam. Any fisherman's creel or boat should have its silverlings of many a kind: incidentally, the word could be a telescoped abbreviation of the 'Silver Darlings', of whom Neil Gunn writes so finely, the herrings that have fed his Scotland, more or less, and made great men of the sea.

SKEIN

THE old nouns of assembly have been kept familiar. The murmuration of starlings, charm of finches, and gaggle of geese are well known. I like, too, a skein of wild-fowl. It suggests so well the white and fleecy flux of gulls and what Ralph Hodgson so rightly called the ribboning of plover in the sky. I came across this usage of skein in one of Seton Gordon's Scottish chronicles, *A Highland Year*, a record of browsing and tramping and bird-watching in our far north-west. 'The most lovely sight of the week was a skein of snow-white whooper swans.' The whoopers inhabit certain Highland fresh-water lochs from October to April. Then they remember the pleasures of Iceland and are off. Seton Gordon saw the skein of swans drifting back to Sutherland across an October sky. They had come 600 miles and were aweary of the trip, moving slowly to its end.

SKELDER

AN old word for swindle and perhaps not remarkable. But I found it in a typical Jonsonian passage, which is worth the quoting. Tucca in 'The Poetaster' is denouncing the players who leave none alone, cartooning here and lampooning there. 'Your courtier cannot kiss his mistress's slippers in quiet for 'em: nor your white innocent gallant pawn his revelling suit to make his punk a supper. An honest, decayed commander cannot skelder, cheat, nor be seen in a bawdy house but he shall be straight in one of their bawdy comedies. They are grown licentious, the rogues, libertines, flat libertines. They forget they are in the statute, the rascals; they are blazon'd there.' So Tucca puts down the harlotry players, statutory vagabonds outside the law. The argument skelders a little, perhaps, but who can question the phrasing of it?

HERE is one of the myriad words which are so commonly used as to be taken for granted, but are queer and exciting when you look behind the letters. Skirmish is the Italian *scaramuccia* and therefore the same as our stage-friend Scaramouch, the boastful poltroon of the Commedia Dell-Arte, a person always threatening to, or beginning to, fight but never going on with the job. The word skirmish went up in the world. One can skirmish bravely and honourably now: the implied caution can be commendable. Scaramouch, on the other hand, fell even lower and the character-title of the wordy coward, continually mocked and beaten by Harlequin, became a term for any kind of rogue and knave.

I have elsewhere commented on the way in which certain letters, or combinations of letters, become associated with certain qualities: 'l' is the initial of most terms for lust, lechery, lewdness and so on: 'st' introduces the strong, stout, stubborn stalwarts: 'sl' gives us slottery, slobbery, slippery, slimy conditions: 'sc' is especially favoured for the tribe of scaramouch, the scamps and scoundrels, the scurvy knaves whom Shakespeare called 'scroyles'. The last war added scrounger to the list of scald, scabby, scruffy, scrimshankers and scelerate practitioners of skulduggery. Scald, by the way, is Elizabethan for scabby and generally implied more than physical blemish or filth, as lousy does now. The two were linked by Fluellen in describing Pistol, 'the rascally, scald, peggarly, lousy, pragging knave'! Robert Greene, destitute, dropsical, and dying, had railed at some of his fellow-writers, 'Shake-scene' included, in his 'Groatsworth of Wit'. This provoked Nashe to deny that he had had any hand in the business. In his preface to *Pierce Penniless* he protested,

> Other news I am advised of, that a scald trivial lying pamphlet, called Greene's 'Groatsworth of Wit', is given out to be my doing. God never have care of my soul, but utterly renounce me, if the least word or syllable in it proceed from my pen.

Scrub, as an adjective for paltry or mean, is now mainly applied to live-stock: scrub bulls are contrasted with pedigree champions and I have seen German second-grade troops described by a war-correspondent as scrub when compared with Panzer Grenadiers. There are occasional exceptions to the rule that 'sc' is a bad start. (I have alluded to scrumptious already.) But on the whole Captain Scaramouch goes skirmishing at the head of scurvy scapegrace scullions, the scum and scourings of society.

SLUMMOCKY AND WOMMACKY

SLUMMOCK, for a cheeky slut, and slummocky for untidy, impudently careless, or shambling of gait lack dictionary status, but they are too good to be missed and seem to be fairly widespread in plebeian speech. If slummocky, why not wommacky which has been sent me from Oldham? This comes from a correspondent in that city,

> Do you know the word 'wommacky', which seems to mean squeamish and shakey, as after an illness? 'He's been playin' 'im a week and 'e's gone back to 'is work to morn but 'e's nobbut wommacky.' It sounds like a compound of wonky and stomach, doesn't it? I think it is West Riding rather than pure Lanca-shire. Do you know the peculiar use of the word 'hurry' for any kind of an attack of illness, or an exacerbation of illness? To have a hurry, in Oldham, means any kind of attack but has nothing whatever to do with hurrying. 'One o' them funny hurries' is epilepsy, which may also be described as a 'mazy bout'.

Mr. H. J. Massingham has sent me the spelling 'slommacky' as Cotswold English for a devil-may-care attitude. Slummock is also used as a verb in certain parts, to slummock along being to slouch along. Kipling wrote of the drunk man in 'Brugglesmith', the man with a 'carnelian neb', that 'his speech began to slur and slide and slummock'.

English dialect and English family slang is full of rich inventions for slatterns. I have been sent, for example, shandylabbit, and several others. Words for untidy, as I have just said, usually begin with 's' and have a following 'l' somewhere; slummocks are in the company of slinking sluts, slouching slatterns, and sloppy slobberers as well as of shandylabbits. To slubber is Shakespearean for 'make a mess of'. Slubberdegullion is a seventeenth-century word of abuse for slummocky folk.

SPRENT

SPRENT, past participle of the obsolete sprenge for sprinkle, is still just alive. To use it now savours of affectation. It lingered in the classic types of English verse: brown hair was apt to be sprent with grey in the more ambitious schoolboy's renderings of Aeschylus or Euripides. 'The cheek grown thin, the brown hair sprent with grey', in Arnold's 'Thyrsis' set the example. Wordsworth as well as Milton have meadows besprent with flowers and dew. Sprent occurs in a poem of John Clare's and the passage is so vivid, so simple, so perfectly 'Clare-ish' that one is glad to have an excuse for quoting it.

> To note on hedgerow baulks, in moisture sprent,
> The jetty snail creep from the mossy thorn,
> With earnest head, and tremulous intent,
> Frail brother of the morn,
> That from the tiny bent's dew-misted leaves
> Withdraws his timid horn,
> And fearful vision weaves.

I owe a reminder of this passage to my late friend and colleague on the *Saturday Review*, T. Earle Welby, whose *Silver Treasury of English Lyrics* revealed in brief the width of reading and the range of taste which his larger works and genial company confirmed in full.

SWAN

GEORGE MEREDITH once used swan as a verb, but he found
no support until the Army's 'armour' took it up to signify a tank's
uninterrupted progress or dalliance. 'We were just swanning
round', wrote a British Captain on the easy capture of Lille in
September, 1944. To swan is a term of grace which some may
think too delicate for a tank. But there it is, a happy recruit to the
verbs derived from the names of birds and animals, like the Shakespearean 'to spaniel', for fawning, or the universal 'to duck' for
bobbing down. To hawk has developed a curious company of
meanings: a hawker is one who peddles things or clears his throat
or keeps falcons to go 'a-birding'. The seeming ecstasy of the lark
has been degraded to the service of ragging and practical joking.
Fops can be said to peacock and tanks, as we saw, to swan. It is odd
that the R.A.F. do not appear to have used many avian metaphors.
The planes stooged around while the tanks were, more poetically,
swanning.

After writing this note I was introduced, through a 'Torque-
mada' cross-word, to mallemaroking, which means the visiting and
carousing of sailors of the Greenland vessels. This very old word,
with its limited range (why only Greenland?), is explained by
Chambers as being derived from mallemuck or mallemoke, the
fulmar petrel. The motion of carousing parties, Greenland-way,
was reminiscent of the petrel's dipping flight. As tanks now swan,
so sailors mallemucked or mallemaroked. Returning to the swan,
the bird and word float handsomely on English lakes and letters.
By one of the curious sports of language the swan, because he was
alleged to sing only at the point of death, became the playful English
for a poet whose very life is song. So Vergil was the Mantuan swan
and Shakespeare Avon's.

It is impossible to imagine an English summer without swans;
they ride our poetry down the ages as they still bedeck our ponds;
they were the escorts of royal barges on the Tudor Thames, and
there, royal property and common ornament, they still abide. To

the Jew of old they were merely unclean; the Bible spoke of them but once, and that to avert the appetite. They were ranked with the scavenging birds and cooks were forbidden to bring them to table. But to the pagan Greek the swan was Olympian company and even a divine disguise; to Christian England he became a symbol of purity.

> Fowls so lovely that they sure did deem
> Them heavenly born

is a reminder not only that the American usage of the word 'sure' is good Spenserian English, but that Spenser put the swan in the most exalted corner of the avian catalogue:

> For sure they did not seeme
> To be begot of any earthly Seede,
> But rather Angels or of Angel's breede.

Like the Greeks, we almost deified swans aforetime — but now we match them with machines.

SWANKY

T H I S from Gavin Bone on Anglo-Saxon poetry: 'It is the strange consonant combinations of which we have no specimens in modern English which seem to us savage and uncouth. For instance, "wl" at the beginning of a word, e.g. Wlanc, which seems as odd as the "ng" at the beginning of some African words, or "sth", "shth" at the end of a verb. Actually "wlanc" (pronounced with its "a" far back) is a splendid word for its meaning, which is "proud". We have felt the advantage of such a word in modern English and have con-scribed "swanky" from one of the dialects. "Wlanc" is a more serious word, but with the good elements of "swanky".'

The dialect from which swanky was 'conscribed' was his own Scottish. The swanky lad is not a figure of up-to-date pavement slang imported from the U.S.A., but a Scottish 'jo' of considerable antiquity. Mourning the Scottish dead ('The English, for ance, by guile wan the day') Jane Elliot wrote in her farewell to the lads 'cauld in the clay', of whom all Scotland was 'wlanc':

> At e'en in the gloaming, nae swankies are roaming,
> 'Bout stacks with the lasses at bogle to play:
> But ilk maid sits drearie, lamenting her dearie —
> The Flowers of the Forest are a' wede away.

A game of Bogle must have been a kind of Bogey-Bogey romp, bogle being a spectre, bug-bear, or scare-crow.

SWASH

'GREGORY, remember thy swashing blow.' So was the servant tarred on to battle in the brawling of the Capulets and Montagues. Swashing. It is a good, rich word. The braggart swashed his buckler and the brave man swashed his foe. In the Lexicon we come also to slams, swipes, slashes, sloshes, and slogs. Swipe, perhaps, is the best of them, but the word has been insulted by its application (in the plural) to the feeblest tipple, whereas it should obviously be kept for the strongest. It emerges from all this that we insist upon a sibilant to give the effect of a descending blow; there are swash, swipe, swish, and swat; smite, slog, and slam. The biffs and bashes and beats and batters must take second place in this contest of alliterative violence. For my part, I find the antique swash a better word than any of the modern variants and regret its disappearance. Cricketer, remember thy swashing blow.

The swash may not be a cricketer's stroke, either as a stylist's joy or a business proposition. But in a stylish innings the mixture of a swash, like the mixture of a lie elsewhere, doth ever add pleasure. We want neither a day's cricket that is all swashing nor a day's cricket that has no swash at all. We enjoy the batsman who has seen some tip of roof or tree and made it his target for the day because it caught his eye and stirred his spirit. Every well-appointed cricket ground ought to have a swasher's mark, like Parr's elm at Trent Bridge or the Pavilion at Lord's or the duck-pond at the far end of the village green. Water has an especial fascination for all proud and persistent swashers. A river should meander round the country cricket-field and glitter with enticement for the batsmen. The Eden-girt field at Appleby in Westmorland, that gem of county towns, must be a splendid lure to the smiter of half-volleys. A proper end of a swash is a splash.

The golfer has been told a hundred times and knows full well that it is silly to 'press', that strength is not length, that swashing will only add fifty yards to his slice or his pull, and that it will cost him the hole for the fun of laying-on. But swash he heartily will, at least from time to time. For among the major pleasures of life is that of a mighty slog or swipe. Golfing in Denmark I found that Stroke Play was *slaeg-spiel* (slaeg is pronounced something like slay) which pleased me. The British sentiment is all for smallness; we prefer David to Goliath, though giants cannot help their size. Still, we do like a big man hitting hugely, whatever the game. (Is billiards an exception? Not always, in the simpler reaches of that sport.) So may a man 'punce it', as they say in Lancashire shrewdly, for punce is a good word. Let him knock the cover off the ball: let him swash.

TAWDRY

TAWDRY is a cousin of Tantony, the latter, as I noted, being a shortened version of St. Antony and applied to the smallest pig of a litter. Tawdry, in the same way, is St. Audrey and began its new life as a piece of lace. 'Come,' says Mopsa, in *The Winter's Tale*, 'you promised me a tawdry-lace and a pair of sweet gloves.' It is obvious from this that there was nothing tawdry about the original tawdry-lace: it was a covetable article. The usual explanation is that St. Audrey believed herself to be punished for wearing rich jewellery round her neck: accordingly she took to wearing a collar of fine lace as a precautionary and ethical device. The tawdry-lace of the sixteenth and seventeenth century was a treasured article and Wycherley could call a Tawdry Rogue 'well-dressed', but it began to decline in quality, became showy, and was linked with cheap

133

vanity. Hence our own adjective tawdry. St. Antony is hardly insulted by association with a nice little pig: but we have been certainly treating St. Audrey with injustice. Another view is that tawdry came from the gew-gaws sold at Ely Fair on St. Audrey's Day. And what of gew-gaw? The learned say it is a duplicated form of 'gifan' to give, the impolite suggestion of this being that presents are usually trash. Anyhow it is no bad term of contempt, and Dryden made it an effective adjective.

> Give to your boy, your Caesar,
> This rattle of a globe to play withal,
> This gew-gaw world.

Gew-gaw never had any favourable aspect, but tawdry's youth was even saintly.

THRUMBLE

COMING across the character of Bullithrumble in the works of the Elizabethan dramatist Greene, I naturally attributed the first part of the word to the bully boy whose adjective has lived down the ages. But thrumble? Thrumbling is crowding, amassing, heaping together. A Bullithrumble should be a go-getter, a scrounger, perhaps even a miser. An Elizabethan translator of Plutarch talked of 'Wicked and lewde folke, who gather, thrumble, and heape together all sorts of gaine'. Thrumble has also been used as an intransitive verb for press or crowd. Perhaps 'muscle in' is the modern equivalent for the lady 'who thrumbleth and thrusteth in at the gates of heaven'. Such thrumbling abounds in war-time travel; the other, acquisitive thrumbling is also a war-time occurrence, especially where public funds and property are concerned. When money flows like water, there will be many to thrumble to it. I have also found thrumble for thumb or strum in Restoration comedy. The strings of guitars were thrumbled: so, likewise, were the heart-strings of the ladies.

TINKLE

'GIVE me a tinkle', says the modern, inviting telephony. It is a gentle word for a ring, its derivation obviously coming from the sound of metal lightly struck. Yet tinkle has occurred in tremendous passages. Isaiah for example, explained that,

> Because the daughters of Zion are haughty and walk with stretched forth necks and wanton eyes, walking and mincing as they go, and making a tinkling with their feet,

the Lord would smite these ladies with scabs on the scalp and other physical penalties. The offence given was due to their gauds, catalogued as follows: Bravery of tinkling ornaments about their feet, cauls (hair-nets), round tires like the moon, chains, bracelets, mufflers, bonnets, ornaments of the legs, head-bands, tablets, ear-rings, rings, nose-jewels, changeable suits of apparel, mantles, wimples, crisping-pins, glasses, fine linen, hoods, and veils. On the whole, these tinklers of Zion seem to have been well-equipped vessels of vanity.

Hence tinkling, especially of cymbals, became the special token of vain performance.

> A crowd is not company and faces are but a gallery of pic-tures and talk but a tinkling cymbal where there is not love.

Milton echoes that judgment of Bacon,

> Speaking of human frailty and vanity, we are but crackt cymbals, we do but tinckle.

Tinkling has always seemed to me too small, too dismissive a term for the melody of church-bells heard across country. Theirs is very different music from the jingle of anklets so obnoxious to Isaiah. But it has been beautifully used of sheep-bells. Everybody knows,

> Now fades the glimmering landscape on the sight,
> And all the air a solemn stillness holds,
> Save where the beetle wheels his droning flight,
> And drowsy tinklings lull the distant folds.

Gray redeemed tinkling from the company to which the grave moralists condemned it.

Presumably a tinker was so-called because of the tink-tink he made when mending pots and pans. The Scottish form of tinker, which is tinkler, emphasizes the name's origin among the appropriate music of that craft. In Scotland tinkler, when abbreviated to tink, became a term of contempt. 'Just brute tinks!' Isaiah, so contemptuous of tinkling in ladies, would have seen the point.

Who wrote,

> Nor in obscurèd purlieus would he seek
> For curlèd Jewesses with ankles neat,
> Who, as they walked abroad, made tinkling with their feet?

The answer is John Keats.

TORMENTIL

SYLVIA LYND is a poetess who agrees with Kipling that our flowers sing themselves into a stanza. Torment is an ugly matter, but Tormentil takes the eye and the ear.

> Silverweed and Tormentil,
> And the white Daisy path that stretches
> A milky way over the hill,
> (Yellow in June with Horse-shoe Vetches).

The lines suggest a familiar summer landscape, shimmering surge of fields beneath a June sun, the distance hazy, with all the magic and the mystery of 'over the hills and far away' gently suggested in a misty horizon. Tormentil is 'a low-growing rosaceous herb of trailing habit, common on heaths and dry pastures'. The root is astringent, medicinal, and used in tanning. The reason of the name is dismissed as obscure, but a link with torment is suggested. Torment? Tanning? Schoolboys will not think the union strange.

TRENTAL

TRENTAL, more odd than beautiful, can mean several things connected with thirty, especially a commemoration service held thirty days after burial. So it came to be loosely used for a dirge or lamentation. Herrick in 'The Funeral Rites of the Rose', describes how

> The holy sisters, some among,
> The sacred dirge and trental sung,

and adds:

> At last, when prayers for the dead
> And rites were all accomplishèd,
> They, weeping, spread a lawny loom,
> And closed her up as in a tomb.

This is worth quoting in order to remind the modern ear that prayer was once pronounced as what it is, a word of two syllables. But, in England, how often now? In Scotland the roll of the r's will help to keep the syllables distinct, but in C. of E. diction one expects an offering of prah — and very often gets it.

UPSY

THIS suggests tipsy and was, in fact, frequently connected with toping. The Jacobeans were used to drinking 'Upsy Dutch' which meant heavily; but only because the Dutch were esteemed to be sturdy potmen. Upsy, in fact, means ' in the manner of', being an Anglicized form of 'op zijn'. Upsy could be, and was, later on applied to other matters than Dutch and drink. Both love-making and cooking could be Upsy French. In the seventeenth century a wooer could have praised his flower-like mistress as being 'fair upsy daisy'; but our upsidaisy is defined as a variant of up-a-daisy, an exclamation used in lifting a child that has tumbled.

USKY

THE Gaels' 'Uisge Beatha' (water of life), is familiar to us by the rather mean name of whisky. It first became usquebaugh and by 1770 the English were calling it (and calling for it) by the word we now know. But, for a while, in the early eighteenth century, when Wade's men were exploring and road-building in the Highlands, the term hovered in an intermediate stage as Usky, a stage which has its own suitability and attraction. Usky was the spelling used, for example, by Edmund Burt, an officer of engineers who wrote letters from the North of Scotland about 1730, explaining the deeds and pleasures of the natives. They give, he said, to their children of six or seven years as much usky at a nip as would fill a wine-glass. Evidently this strengthened young heads and stomachs for the serious drinking of later years. When some of Burt's fellow-officers audaciously entered upon an usky-drinking-match with the locals, the Highlanders were easy victors and left the field without loss, whereas the English casualties were severe. Here is Burt's chronicle of the ruin. 'One of the officers was thrown into a fit of gout, without hopes: another had a most dangerous fever: a third lost his skin and hair by the surfeit.' The fourth competitor went 'yellow' in the slangy modern sense. 'When drunkenness ran high, he took several opportunities to sham it', and so, presumably, preserved his looks, locks, and hide.

It seems to have been a good party on the whole. One has heard of curious effects produced by a carouse, but a case of simultaneous depilation and depellation is new to me and should stand high among the cautionary tales for the reckless practitioners of absorbency. The standard of consumption in the Highlands, as Burt saw them, was imposing. 'Some of the Highland gentlemen', observed this Gael-watcher, not denying them the title of gentry, 'are immoderate drinkers of usky, even three or four quarts at a sitting.' Burt himself was an anti-usky man, believing that 'this spirit has in it, by infusion, the seeds of anger, revenge, and murder (this, I confess is a little too poetical), but those who drink of it to any degree of excess behave, for the most part, like barbarians, I think much beyond the effect of any other liquor'. Life in 'the lone sheiling of the misty island' was not, in those days, dry. The collector of customs at Stornoway told Burt that 'One hundred and twenty families drink yearly 4000 English gallons of this spirit and brandy together, although many of them are so poor that they cannot afford to pay for much of either, which, you know, must increase the quantity drunk by the rest'. Burt did not, however, clinch his argument by relating the statistics of murder to those of usky-gallons drunk. It seems a little odd that 'uisge beatha', the spirit of life, should have been the name for a fluid so lethal. In any case, for the kind of skin-destroying, hair-uprooting tipple that Burt describes, usky seems to be an apter, because a rougher, name than whisky.

There were other spellings. A Scottish Gentleman, who visited the Highlands in 1737, was so delighted by the work of Wade, Burt, and their men in the civilizing of the country that he made his obeisance in a poem of a thousand lines.

> And thee, O Wade, shall coming Ages bless
> Whose prudent Care did give the Scheme Success, etc. etc.

At one of the banquets of celebration given after the building of another Highland bridge, the poet says that the workers

> Then beef and pudding plentifully eat
> With store of cheering Husque to their meat.

He also alludes to the 'Houses of Intertainment' set up for the travellers.

> With Corn and Grass, enclosures all around,
> Where fitt Supplys, for Men and Horse, are found.
> There various Meats and Liquors too are got,
> But Usqueba must never be forgot.

Those travelling over Wade's roads in 1944, as I had the pleasure of doing, at least over part of them, were not so lucky with their meats and liquors. Certainly Usqueba was not forgot; but, no less certainly, it was never as much in the glass as it was in the mind.

VAIL

DOES anybody vail now — in the sense of taking off his hat or making obeisance? Or does anybody 'take a vail' in its old meaning, that of a noun to designate an extra payment or tip? Milton would have understood a waiter or a cab-driver who refused to vail until he got his vail and any eighteenth-century gentleman would have vailed to another who vailed to him — except Pope's Aristarchus (mask for the mighty scholar Bentley),

> His Hat, which never vail'd to human pride,
> Walker with reverence took and laid aside.

Shakespearean monarchs use this word, should occasion come for removal of the hardware hats of their profession,

> None that beheld him, but, like lesser lights,
> Did vail their crowns to his supremacy.

Again time comes for La Pucelle,

> When France must vail her lofty-plumed crest
> And let her head fall into England's lap.

Vailing descended from plumes and coronets to the humbler head-gear of gentry and even commoners. Now that so many wear no hats at all, there is less need than ever for this nice little word, to whose passing form I vail in metaphor.

VAMP

VAMP begins life as a short sock; next it is the front part of a boot which covers the short sock. Thus to vamp boots meant to give them new fronts and later on to mend or patch them in any way. So from boots to books, plays, music, and even ladies. (To vamp a lady in Wycherley's England was not to seduce her but to send her to the doctor that she be repaired.) In general vamping was mending, refurbishing, or, as Whitehall now so cumbrously insists, rehabilitating. Play-texts were vamped up in Jacobean and Restoration times and musical men have been said to vamp when they strummed and played about with old tunes, or even when they improvised new ones. The modern vamp, whose arrival the *O.E.D.* dates at 1922, is short for vampire; that was apparently a word of Magyar origin, meaning a reanimated corpse with a taste for sucking the blood of people asleep. So it was applied to any malignant succubus. The English as well as the Americans have used the word more gently. There used, I believe, to be a North London football team whose members were proud to style themselves the Crouch End Vampires. The ordinary vamp of modern conversation may be a naughty girl, but she hardly merits sharing a name with the medieval horror who broke out of the sepulchre in order to slake a thirst with the gore of snoozing innocents.

WELKIN

T H E Welkin still rings in writing of 'ye olde' kind. But nobody would now use that word seriously. The welkin came to us from the S.E. as weolkne and weolkyn, meaning a cloud. Then the cloud became the arch of heaven and the sky itself. Then, to the all-seizing genius of Shakespeare, it was a sky-blue adjective. I came across it in *The Winter's Tale*: cries Leontes to Mamillius,

> Come, sir page,
> Look on me with your welkin eye: sweet villain!
> Most dear'st: My collop!

(Scots know all about collops from eating them minced. A collop is a slice; so a child, being a slice of life, can be a collop too.)

Poets, when calling the sky the welkin, have as a rule regarded it chiefly as a sounding-board. The welkin does not merely ring. In Marlowe it also howls and cracks. Marlowe, incidentally, in *Tamburlaine* gives a fair anticipation of a flying-bomb aloft:

> As when a fiery exhalation,
> Wrapt in the bowels of a freezing cloud,
> Fighting for passage, makes the welkin crack.

I regret the passing of welkin from the common speech and script of to-day. Especially does the adjectival welkin seem a loss.

After all, we use blue for so many things that another word for this colour would be valuable. 'Feeling a bit welkin this morning?' 'Yes, sir, I'm afraid we kept it up last night till all was welkin.' 'Rough house?' 'Well, some of the stories were a bit welkin.' How hard do we work our blues!

WINKLE

WINKLE, of course, is periwinkle, which either as a flower or as a gastropod mollusc is an attractive word. The soldiers have turned winkle into a verb. The enemy are winkled out of holes and strongholds, as winkles are evicted with a pin. This is picturesque and vivid use of language. W. M. Praed, in his poem on Teignmouth in S. Devon, then wearing a 'rural grace', observed:

> The invalids enjoying dips
> The children launching tiny ships,
> The beldames clothed in rags and wrinkles
> Investigating periwinkles.

Or, as we might say now, winkling out the works.

In the opinion of the late Sir George Sitwell the periwinkle was a charming flower and justly made a term of endearment in the Middle Ages, an honour it shared with 'pig's eye', Chaucer's complimentary way of describing a pretty girl.

WIZEN

THE termination 'ed', so common in English verbs and participles, is a handicap in the appeal to the ear. Especially if the following word begins with a d or t, the accumulation of dentals is a nuisance. 'Distasted with the salt of broken tears' is an exquisite line: but, if Shakespeare had written about salt-distasted tears, the result would have been ugly beyond question. Some participles ending in -en are effective for this very reason and our poets, perhaps more instinctively than of set purpose, are to be found using such a word in order to escape the -ed or a clumsy -ing. Kipling's 'writhen' comes to mind at once. Wizen has been in occasional use for centuries as a replacement for wizened and I came across it anew in a poem by the Irishman F. R. Higgins lamenting the death of a nomad Gaelic bard called Patrick O'Connor,

> They'll miss his heavy stick and stride in Wicklow,
> His story-telling down Winetavern-street,
> Where old men sitting in the wizen daylight
> Have kept an edge upon his gentle wit.

Higgins did well to avoid the two d's in 'wizened daylight'.

WUTHERING

EMILY BRONTË'S 'Wuthering', with its powerfully suggested mixture of weather and bluster, should really become Dictionary English. After all, the name is a piece of authentic dialect. A correspondent writes to me from the Brontës' own town of Haworth,

'The wind wuthers still down a certain street near Haworth Church now called Changegate. It is, or was, known to the ancients as "Down Wutheram". To-day a girl is said to wuther off in a tantrum.'

That tantrum reminds me of another word applied to feminine disgust. 'I am told,' writes a friend, 'that a Master-at-Arms at Southport, in charging a Wren who had been late for duty' (shouldn't he have said 'adrift'?), 'insisted that, "When rebuked, she flounced". He was asked what he meant by flounced and replied, "She made a derisive movement of the 'ips".' Whether you say of recalcitrants that they flounce or wuther off is perhaps mostly a matter of English geography, that blessed geography which, despite all the flattening out of distance by mechanical transport, still retains the counties and parishes as places of different habit and lingo. My correspondent from 'Down Wutheram' (or near it) adds that, thereabouts, you can hear a slippery old customer called 'an old Slaipse Corpse'. It is a good wuthering phrase, with a smack of east wind in it.

ZYMURGY

Is 'Z', as Shakespeare held, an evil superfluity? ('Thou whoreson
Zed! Thou unnecessary letter!') It certainly introduces exquisite
things. Zephyrs sing wooingly through lyrics ancient and modern,
and who can forget Marlowe's Zenocrate?

> Now walk the angels on the walls of heaven,
> As sentinels to warn th'immortal souls,
> To entertain divine Zenocrate.

Having begun this book with reference to Mr. James Bridie let
me end likewise. Somebody once observed of him that it needs
a Glasgow Rationalist to make the best drama out of the Bible: I
do not know whether Bridie subscribes to that title of Rationalist,
but certainly a Tudor poet famed (or at least attacked) for his atheism
made more lovely music out of heaven and even of theology than
did his colleagues, Shakespeare included. Marlowe's Muse it was
who made damned Faustus cry,

> See, see where Christ's blood streams in the firmament,

and that same Muse trod with angels on the walls of heaven in
preparation for divine Zenocrate.

But Z, on the whole, despite attachment to some beauties, seems
to me a dismissive and contemptuous letter, fit for rough or rude
expletives (as in our own Zooks and Zounds and the alien Zut) or
for epithets of dislike and disdain. The dictionary further persuaded
me to this view after I had read in rapid succession, Zopilote, a
kind of carrion vulture, Zoril, a skunk, and Zoster, the disease of
shingles. But in order that this book may not end amid themes
and sounds unpleasant, let me note that the lexicon now before
me (*Shorter O.E.D.*, Two Vols.) finishes with 'Zymurgy', which
means 'the practice or art of fermentation as in wine-making,
brewing, distilling, etc.' We have passed through bad times for
zymurgous men — or, more classically, zymergs — and what little
they could do has helped us much. They make a final and, I think,
effective plea for Shakespeare's 'unnecessary letter'.